Kevin Daniels on the "Pink Crack" (5.11), Boulder Basin, Black Mountain. Photo by Bill Freeman.

SOUTHERN CALIFORNIA

BOULDERING GUIDE

SECOND EDITION

CRAIG FRY

FALCONGUIDES ®

GUILFORD, CONNECTICUT
HELENA, MONTANA
AN IMPRINT OF THE GLOBE PEQUOT PRESS

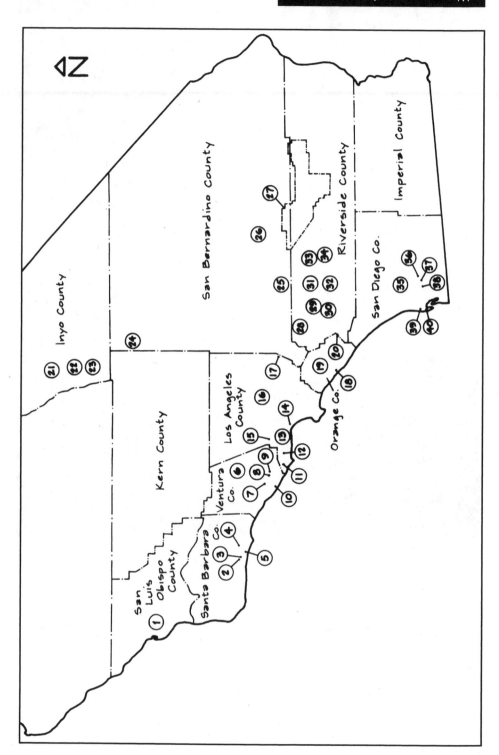

KEY TO INTRODUCTION MAP
Principal Bouldering Areas (Minor areas not shown)

1. Bishop's Peak
2. Lizard's Mouth
3. Brickyard
4. Painted Cave
5. Patterson Wall
6. The Swimming Hole
7. Camarillo Grove Boulder
8. Coyote Beach
9. Gainsborough Boulder
10. Point Mugu
11. Miniholland
12. Malibu Creek
13. Purple Stones
14. Sunset Stones
15. Stoney Point
16. Horse Flats   pp 75
17. Mt. Baldy
18. Corona del Mar
19. Hart Park
20. El Coriso and Ortega Falls

21. Coso Boulders
22. Fossil Falls
23. Black Planets
24. Wagon Wheel
25. Mentone Boulders
26. Giant Rock
27. Joshua Tree National Monument
28. Mt. Rubidoux
29. Bernasconi Ridge
30. Nuevo Areas
31. Beaumont Glue-on Area
32. Hemet Areas
33. Black Mountain
34. Idyllwild Areas
35. Mt. Woodson
36. Magnolia
37. Santee
38. Singing Hills
39. La Jolla Beach
40. Pump Wall

FALCONGUIDES®

Since the first edition of this guide, climbing and bouldering have grown exponentially. With the advent of sport climbing and climbing gyms, climbing has become accessible to a much wider range of people at all levels of fitness. The increased impact on climbing areas puts a new responsibility on the guidebook author in regard to access issues, ratings, and preservation of each area and its history.

The first edition of this guide was a bit of an experiment. I attempted to accumulate as much information as possible from people I met at bouldering areas in order to put together a draft guide of sorts. Once published, climbers could review the guide and then help fill in the blanks, add new areas, and make corrections. Many people have contributed to make this second edition a more complete and updated guide and their help is truly appreciated. However, I suspect that many climbers think a guidebook author is psychic and that route information just seeps in like osmosis, or that the author should contact every climber in the area before publishing, or be required to climb every route in the book to verify its existence and rating. Unfortunately, perfect knowledge of each problem and area is impossible, and putting together a guidebook is more work than you can ever imagine. The author must rely on volunteered information because without new input, it isn't possible to keep up with all of the new development. With that said, I'd like to welcome every climber to contribute to the next edition of this guide. This will help preserve our rich history and provide a means for everybody to have access to new bouldering areas and problems. Additions and corrections to this guide are easily made by making notes on a photocopy of any page and sending it to:

Southern California Bouldering Guide
c/o The Globe Pequot Press
P.O. Box 480
Guilford, CT 06437

This second edition has been completely updated and expanded to include many new areas, including San Luis Obispo and Southern Inyo Counties. Due to access issues, many maps to artificial walls have been eliminated.

TABLE OF CONTENTS

*P*ublishing this guidebook would not have been possible without the help of many peo-ple. I'd like to offer special thanks to the following climbers for generously providing a tremendous amount of information and support:

Ron Amick authored the introductions to San Diego County and Mt. Woodson, and provided huge amounts of information about these areas.

Todd Battey provided photos and much information about Horse Flats, the Nuevo areas, Mt. Rubidoux and San Luis Obispo.

Kerwin Klein provided excellent information, maps and drawings of the Nuevo areas, Black Mountain, and Malibu.

Dean Kubani assisted in the production of the second edition and researched new areas, drew new maps, re-drew old maps, took photos and, with his excellent illustrations, elevated the quality of this guide.

Jon Larson provided the San Luis Obispo drawings and information.

Bill Levanthal contributed a huge amount of information about Stoney Point, Malibu Creek, the Purple Stones, and helped to verify many of the ratings.

Mike Paul, an extraordinary artist in climbing, music, and illustration, graciously allowed the use of his Mt. Woodson guide, and provided much information about Joshua Tree, Black Mountain, and South Ridge.

I'd also like to thank the following people for sending information, photos, support, draw-ings, or just going bouldering and pointing at things:

Rick Allenby, Paul Anderson, Jim Angione, Mike Ayon, John Bachar, Allen Bartlett, Malcom Best, David Bevan, Bob Conklin, Matt Dancy, Steve Edwards, Greg Epperson, Erik Eriksson, Dave Evans, the late Bob Fish, Bill Freeman, Dimitri Fritz, Shane Fry, Damian Gebert, Mari Gingery, Todd Gordon, Darrel Hensel, Jeff Johnson, Neal Kaptain, Dave Katz, Vaino Kodas, Spencer Lennard, John Long, Dan McQuade, Jack Marshall, Troy Mayr, Roger Peck, Kevin Powell, Rob Raker, John Sherman, Dave and Rob Stahl, Bron Stokes, Greg Vernon, Randy Vogel, Mike Waugh and **Chuck Zilm.**

Southern California is well known for its abundant bouldering areas. Many of the areas have been developed into world-class bouldering sites with boulder problems at the highest level of difficulty. This extensive development has led to producing some of the most popular climbing areas in the world, rivaling Hueco Tanks, Fontainbleu, and Yosemite in bouldering excellence. No single area in Southern California would be called the world's best, but taken as a whole, Southern California does offer the largest concentration of developed bouldering to be found anywhere. Southern California offers every type of rock, from slippery granite cracks to overhanging pockets—all within a couple of hours drive of each other. Many of these areas offer more than just bouldering; they are also great escapes from the heat, smog, and urban blight, where climbers can hike, explore, meet friends, or just hang out.

This guide covers all of the major areas from San Luis Obispo to San Diego. Detailed maps of each area give complete information on locating an individual boulder by route name and rating. Some of the bouldering areas also have top-rope and lead routes. These are illustrated in topos and maps if they are not covered in other guidebooks. The selection of bouldering areas and problems covered in this book is by no means exhaustive. At the request of local climbers, several areas were not included. Other areas were left out because of their unappealing nature, lengthy approach, or lack of information. Areas of lesser significance have maps to their locations rather than detailed route information, giving the adventurous many areas to explore and develop.

The convenient access of bouldering in Southern California has led to some of these areas becoming the most popular climbing areas in the region. Many of them are very close to major cities—unlike good roped climbing areas which can take several hours of driving time. Besides accessibility, most climbers are drawn to bouldering for the excitement of doing hard moves, the camaraderie, excellent training, and the freedom from bothersome roped climbing gear. What boulders lack in size, they make up for in difficulty. The art of bouldering has been developed to an extremely high level. In fact, the hardest climbing moves ever done have been accomplished on boulders. Even for the beginner or intermediate climber, bouldering is a valuable training aid in developing strength and technique.

Bouldering may be the purest form of climbing—the freest and the most extreme: just you and the rock. A boulder problem forces you to experience the rock in an intimate way: subtly molding your fingers into the holds, slowly working out a delicate balance over each foot hold, creating an intense mental focus on the sequence you're about to attempt. The boulder problem brings you to a state of being far beyond the mundane—a state that brings you to your limits, then allows you to exceed them. It is this mental state that has allowed boulder problems to be climbed that defy explanation. For the master, his or her best effort takes more than just putting together a couple of moves; it is an act of brilliance which is seldom if ever repeated.

RATINGS

The difficulty ratings used in this book are a combination of the Yosemite Decimal System (YDS), and the B System, which was developed by John Gill specifically for hard bouldering. These are the most popular bouldering rating systems used in Southern California.

The purpose of a rating system is to place an objective value onto a climbing situation. However, the inherent problem of any rating system lies in the fact that every climbing situation will be different for each climber and each attempt. Due to these problems with rating, no system has been devised that can accurately rate a boulder problem. Since there is no way to achieve a perfect system, we must settle for a system that will give us a general estimate of difficulty. Short of saying "hard," "harder," or "hardest," the ratings used in this book should be thought of as an approximation of difficulty.

Another factor worth noting is that boulder problems have traditionally been rated on a downgrading principle. In other words, moves that would receive a 5.12 rating on a roped lead might only get a 5.11 rating on a boulder problem. Many other considerations go into the rating, including the pump factor, the sustained nature of the moves, and the fall potential. Although every attempt has been made to assign the most accurate rating possible, I could not personally confirm every rating in this book.

The B System is used to rate boulder problems that are 5.12 and above. This system was developed by John Gill in the early 1960s to fill in the missing ratings of the Yosemite Decimal System, which back then topped out at 5.10. Originally, B1 indicated a boulder problem that was 5.11 or harder. B2 indicated a boulder problem that was considerably more difficult than a B1 problem; and B3 was an even harder problem, so difficult, in fact, that only one person had ever succeeded in climbing it. If any B3 problem was ever repeated, the rating was automatically downgraded to B2. Since John Gill's time, the standard of difficulty has progressed, as has the YDS, and B1 has been transformed into the standard "very hard" problem, equalling 5.12. B2 has come to equal the hardest problems (5.14) done at this time—problems that are seldom repeated. It appears that these days, no one dares call anything B3 for fear of its being downrated. This being the case, most hard problems get lumped into the B1 category. A B1 rating should therefore indicate that the boulder problem is incredibly hard and will require a dedicated effort for success. **See the Rating Comparison Table for a comparison of the rating system used in this book to all other rating systems used in Southern California.**

In this book, hard boulder problems usually done without ropes use the B System, and problems easier than 5.12 use the YDS. Climbs that are commonly led or top-roped also use the YDS and an indication as to whether they are either a lead or a top-rope (TR).

SERIOUSNESS RATINGS

Seriousness ratings are used to give an indication of the potential fall factor and the height of the boulder. Most climbers can usually judge for themselves if a particular problem is over their head, so the lack of a seriousness rating does not necessarily indicate a non-serious problem. The seriousness rating is given to problems that were established without ropes or are routinely done without ropes by expert boulderers. This does not mean a rope should never be employed, since a top-rope can quickly be installed on almost any problem to inspire confidence.

OTD - Off the deck, committing moves near the top of a high boulder

R - Committing moves off the deck with bad landing potential, more difficult and scarier than OTD

X - Probable injury or even death from falling

QUALITY RATINGS

A single star (★) is used to designate exceptional routes and boulder problems. The routes with stars are the best for an area in terms of quality of the rock, the aesthetic appeal and the excellence of the moves required. Each bouldering area has different qualities and the star ratings are not intended for comparison between areas. Also, routes with no stars could be great routes, but perhaps we forgot to give them a star.

RATING COMPARISON TABLE

SOUTHERN CALIFORNIA BOULDERING GUIDE RATING SYSTEM

YDS	SPECIFIC	VAGUE	VERY VAGUE	V-SYSTEM	JT-SYSTEM
5.6	5.6	5.6	5.6		5.6
5.7	5.7	5.7	5.7		5.7
5.8	5.8	5.8	5.8		5.8
5.9-	5.9-	5.9	5.9		5.9
5.9	5.9	5.9	5.9		5.9
5.9+	5.9+	5.9	5.9		5.9
5.10a	5.10a	5.10-	5.10		5.10-
5.10b	5.10b	5.10	5.10		5.10
5.10c	5.10c	5.10	5.10		5.10
5.10d	5.10d	5.10+	5.10	V0	5.10+
5.11a	5.11a	5.11-	5.11	V1	A-
5.11b	5.11b	5.11	5.11	V2	A
5.11c	5.11c	5.11	5.11	V2	A
5.11d	5.11d	5.11+	5.11	V3	A+
5.12a	B1-	B1-	B1	V4	B-
5.12b	B1-	B1	B1	V5	B
5.12c	B1	B1	B1	V5	B
5.12d	B1	B1	B1	V6	B+
5.13a	B1+	B1	B1	V7	C-
5.13b	B1+/B2-	B1+/B2-	B1	V8	C
5.13c	B2-	B2-	B2	V8	C
5.13d	B2	B2	B2	V9	C+
5.14a	B2	B2	B2	V9	D-
5.14b	B2+	B2	B2	V10	D
5.14c	B2+	B2+	B2	V11	D
5.14d	B2+/B3	B2+/B3	B2/B3	V12	D+

TOP-ROPING

Top-ropes are a generally accepted means of protecting short climbs and boulder problems. Anchors are often not present on the tops of boulders, so the anchor rope must be dropped down the opposite side and anchored to a tree, adjacent boulder, or whatever can be found. It is easiest to have two short ropes: one for the anchor and one to use as the top-rope.

BOLTS AND ETHICS

Since this guide covers such a wide range of climbing areas, the subject of bolting ethics cannot be adequately addressed. Sport climbing has diverged from traditional climbing concepts of where and when bolts should be placed. Generally speaking, bolts should only be placed where appropriate and legal. Bolts should not be placed for protection on boulders that are usually done ropeless by more skilled climbers. Use a top-rope instead. The bolting issue appears to be slowly passing from the hands of climbers and entering the domain of land policy makers. Consult the Access Fund for current laws that apply regarding bolting.

Chipping holds, graffiti, or doctoring the rock is neither accepted nor tolerated in any form throughout Southern California. Regarding trash, climbers should not leave it behind, including tape!

BOULDER AND OUTDOOR WALL MAINTENANCE

The maintenance of boulder problems and buildering walls is a topic of concern in Southern California due to the increasing number of climbers. Maintenance and clean-up is required by each of us if we expect to enjoy these areas in the future. Of primary concern is graffiti and caked-on chalk. On concrete walls, graffiti should be painted over with a neutral shade of paint, using a brush or a roller. Natural rock should be sandblasted or paint-stripped. If graffiti is not controlled by climbers, the governing officials will conduct their usual method of control, which is to paint over everything, including the climbing holds. To removed caked-on chalk, use a nylon bristle brush. A wire brush will polish holds and should not be used. Solvents like acetone or alcohol will help remove the chalk.

Another maintenance concern is broken holds. Considerations must be given to take appropriate action in each case of a broken hold. Some holds that break off are better left off, while others must be replaced. On natural rock, friable edges and broken holds have been glued back on or reinforced. This is a touchy subject, and as a rule it is usually considered unethical—illegal in some areas—but a consensus should be sought in each situation. Use PC-7 paste epoxy for reattaching, reinforcing, or constructing artificial walls (available at industrial hardware supply stores).

ACCESS PROBLEMS

Maintaining access to the rocks we climb is becoming increasingly important. Likewise, the responsibility for preventing or solving access problems lies with every climber. All of the rocks described in this book lie on lands that have some administrative watchdog (whether it be governmental or simply a private landowner) who decides whether climbing is an appropriate activity for their land. Minimizing environmental impact and limiting activity that could affect access will help prevent problems and keep the rocks available. The Access Fund is the climber's best resource in dealing with access problems. They can negotiate, organize, and even litigate closures of climbing areas. In addition, should litigation fail, the Access Fund provides the money to purchase or preserve problem areas. Your contribution to the Access Fund is a concrete way of giving something back to climbing. You can make a real difference in the effort to save the rich diversity of climbing resources throughout the United States. The Access Fund publishes a quarterly newsletter that can be received by making a donation of any amount to: The Access Fund, P. O. Box 17010, Boulder, CO 80308.

HOW TO USE THIS GUIDE

This guide is arranged from north to south, and from west to east (with the exception of Southern Inyo County, placed after Orange County). **The map in the front of the book** gives the scope of areas covered, though only the major areas are shown. Chapters are broken down into counties, with all areas covered in each county shown on the initial county map. Each climbing area is shown in maps of increasing detail: an initial map for access, overview maps of the boulders themselves, and finally by topos (side views). Overview maps are used by locating landmarks like roads and rocks, then orienting the north arrow. Then proceed in the desired direction to the route of your choice.

Caution: Not all landmarks and boulders are drawn. Boulder locations and direction may be skewed, relationships to other boulders may be off, and distances may not be to scale with other boulders in the same drawing. Some searching and improvisation may be required.

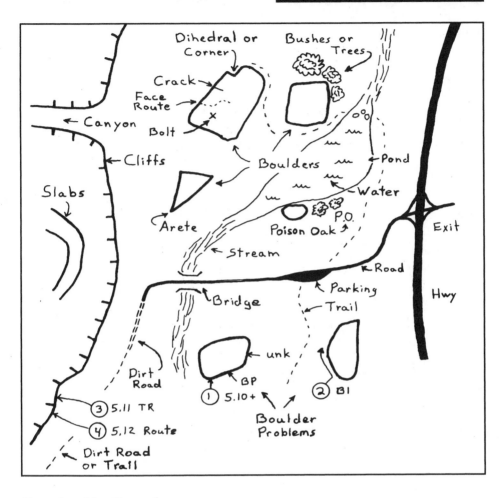

Overview Map Example:

1. Boulder problem 5.10+
2. Traverse problem B1
3. Top-rope route 5.11
4. Leadable route 5.12

Other notation used on overview and topo maps:

BP	Boulder problem—may be any of the following: insignificant; no generally accepted rating; rating unknown; may not go
unk	Unknown boulder problem—may or may not go
TR	Top-rope route
thin	Thin crack or seam
lb	Lieback
chim	Chimney

hand	Hand crack
face	Face climbing
dyno	Dynamic moves; lunge
Yabo start	Start on lowest possible holds—aka as a sit-down start.
Largo start	A jumping dyno used to gain high starting holds.
Cheatstone	A stone placed at the base to enable the climber to reach higher starting holds. May or may not be required.
OTD, R, or X	Seriousness ratings. **See page 3.**
★	Designates a quality route or boulder problem.

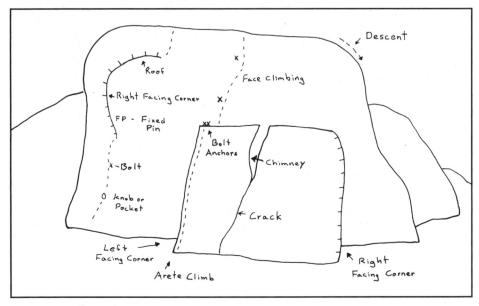

Topo Map Example

Tips for Safe Bouldering

- Clear away all rubble at the base.
- Check out possible descents before you get on top of large boulders.
- Take a look at the top moves to see if you are going for jugs or having to crank a slippery mantle.
- If the base has a bad landing, practice downclimbing the lower section before you get in over your head.
- Hard moves can be worked out by visualizing yourself doing the sequence.
- Use a spotter to help soften the landing, and keep your head from hitting the ground.

There is only one major natural bouldering area in San Luis Obispo County—**Bishop's Peak**. However, there are some artificial wall climbing areas that are quite popular in downtown San Luis Obispo. Consult local climbers for information.

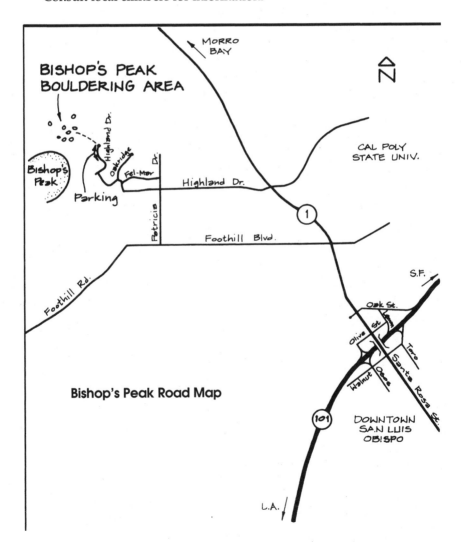

Bishop's Peak Road Map

BISHOP'S PEAK

The bouldering at Bishop's Peak has long been a favorite area for locals and climbers traveling on the 101. The location provides quick access and an intense finger workout. The rock is a very fine grain andesite from a row of ancient volcanos, **Morro Rock** being the last of them above water. The area is characterized by small- to medium-sized edges on vertical to slightly overhanging faces with very good flat landings.

The Potato (no topo) is a 40-foot rock with about eight top rope routes from 5.7 to 5.12. Climbing is good all year long except during and after rain. Poison oak is very abundant and to get to **Boulder in the Woods** you have to walk right through it. Visit the Granite Stairway in San Luis Obispo for more information on Bishop's Peak and outlying areas.

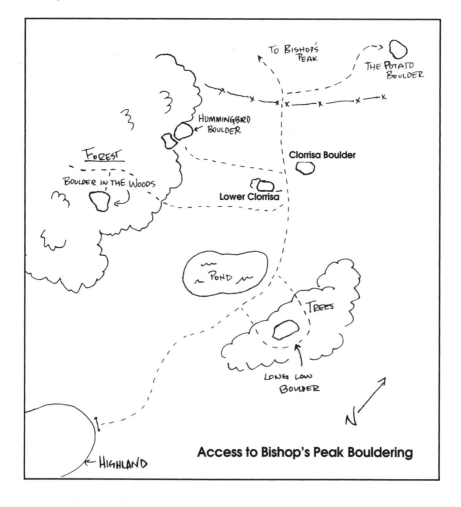

Access to Bishop's Peak Bouldering

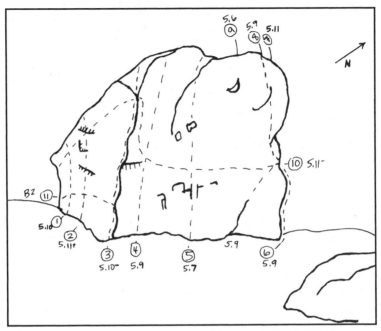

Clorissa Boulder
1. **Mantel 5.10**
2. **Mushies 5.11+/B1- ★**
3. **Corner 5.10-**
4. **Over the Falls 5.9**
5. **5.7**
6. **Helmet 5.9** Many Variations.
7. **Pinky Pockets 5.11 ★**
   Avoids large holds to either side.
8. **5.9**
9. **5.6**
10. **Traverse of Clorissa 5.11- ★**
11. **Low Traverse B2**

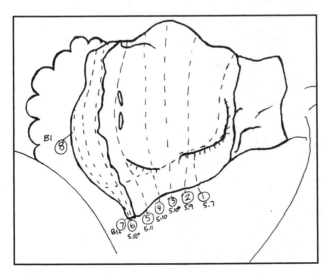

Lower Clorissa Boulder
1. **5.7**
2. **5.9**
3. **Credit Card 5.10+**
4. **Africa Flake 5.10 ★**
5. **Overhanging Corner 5.11**
6. **5.10+**
7. **Pete's Problem B1+** Yabo Start.
8. **Ryan Traverse B1**

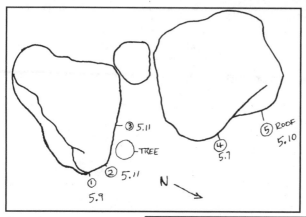

Hummingbird Boulder
1. **5.9**
2. **5.11**
3. **5.11**
4. **5.7**
5. **5.10**

Boulder in the Woods
1. **Sharp Arête 5.8 R★**
   Either side.
2. **Tall Face 5.11 ★**
3. **Rock and Roll Solution 5.10+**
4. **5.7**
5. **5.8**
6. **5.10a**
7. **5.10b**
8. **5.6**
9. **5.8**
10. **Arête 5.10+ ★**
11. **Mercury B2**
    Elimination of arêtes.

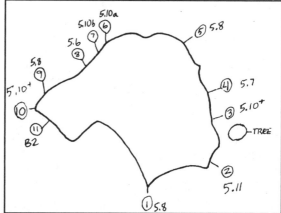

David Bevin on "The Tall Face" (5.11), Boulder in the Woods, Bishop's Peak.

Santa Barbara County offers four main bouldering areas. The hills above Santa Barbara are covered with sandstone outcroppings, but the chaparral-choked approaches have limited the development of new areas to the most adventurous. The primary appeal of the areas described is easy access.

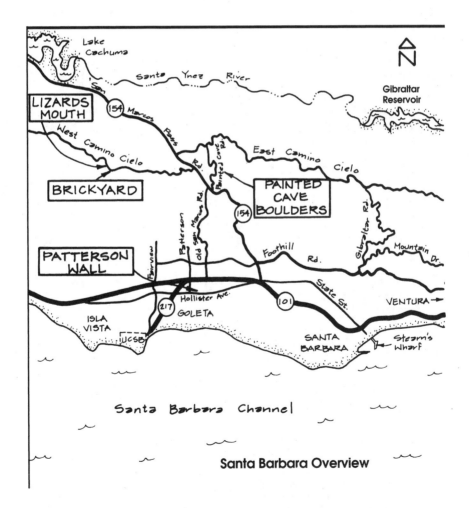

Santa Barbara Overview

LIZARD'S MOUTH AND THE BRICKYARD

These excellent areas consist of scattered sandstone boulders and out-croppings on a scenic ridge overlooking Santa Barbara. **Lizard's Mouth** offers several very good bouldering traverses, a top-rope wall, and a couple of good boulder problems. **Meilee** (5.11 +) is one of the finest boulder traverses in the area. Lizard's Mouth is also very popular with sightseers and partiers—trash and broken glass are abundant.

The Brickyard is a newly-developed bouldering area located just before Lizard's Mouth, and is aptly named because of the red sandstone for-mations stacked in tight arrays, similar to a brickyard. The area offers a variety of face routes, all with a similar lack of positive summit holds. This has spurred the development of the "Brickyard Technique" to protect the climber on high boulder problems. The climber hangs a short piece of rope with knots or a daisy chain from the summit bolts. When the ropeless climber approaches the dicey summit moves, he clips his harness into the hanging rope and moves it up a knot at a time. This technique is only recommended for expert climbers.

Both areas are only partially developed and are great for exploring. A machete and an adventurous attitude will be required to unlock these areas' fullest bouldering potential, although the nearby gun clubs can be an irritating distraction.

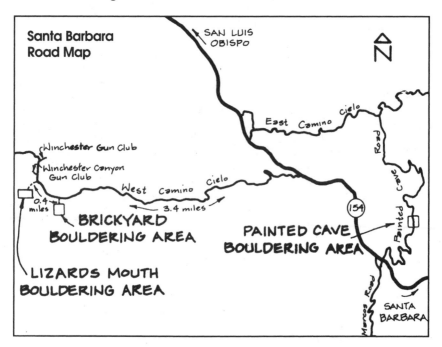

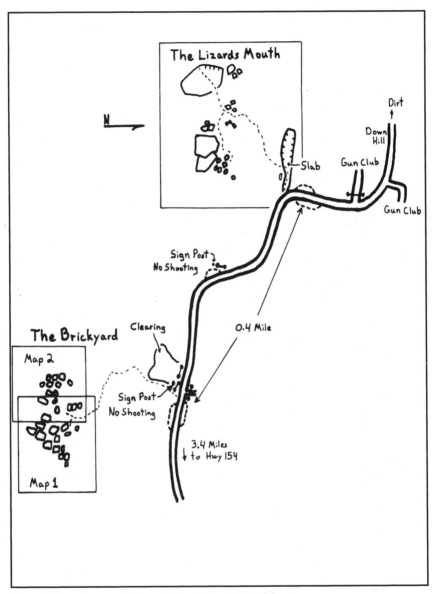

Lizard's Mouth and The Brickyard Access Map

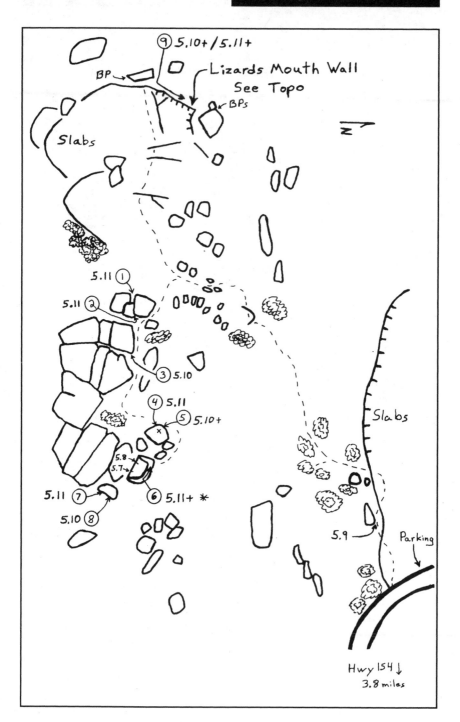

Lizard's Mouth Area

1. **Todd's Problem 5.11**
   Undercling traverse
   black overhang and
   transfer to adjoining
   boulder.
2. **The Lizard's Pit 5.11**
   Sit-down start to
   sandy hueco lunges
   on south boulder.
3. **The Lizard Spine 5.10**

4. **Return of the Fly 5.11**
   TR
5. **Lord of the Flies
   5.10+** TR
6. **Meilee 5.11+ ★**
   Traverse from left to
   right in low cave.
7. **Butthead 5.11** Long
   reach from low start.
8. **Beavis 5.10**

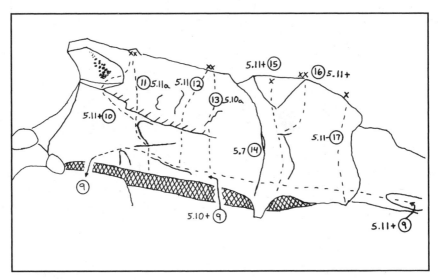

Lizard's Mouth, Wall Topo

9. **The Lizard's Mouth Traverse
   5.10+/5.11+ ★** 5.10+ if started
   at You Skink; 5.11+ if started
   at far right side.
10. **Lizard's Lips 5.11+** TR
11. **Flight of the Iguana 5.11a ★** TR

12. **Gila Monster 5.11** TR
13. **Yellow Belly 5.10a** TR
14. **You Skink 5.7**
15. **Lizard King 5.11+** TR
16. **El Gecko 5.11+ ★** TR
17. **Lizard Music 5.11-** TR

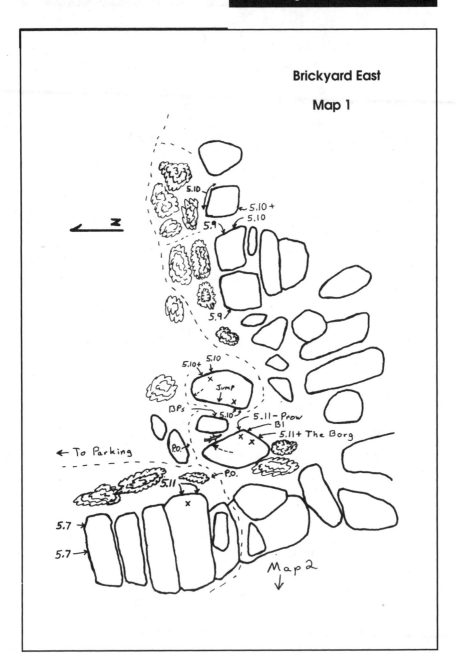

Brickyard East

Map 1

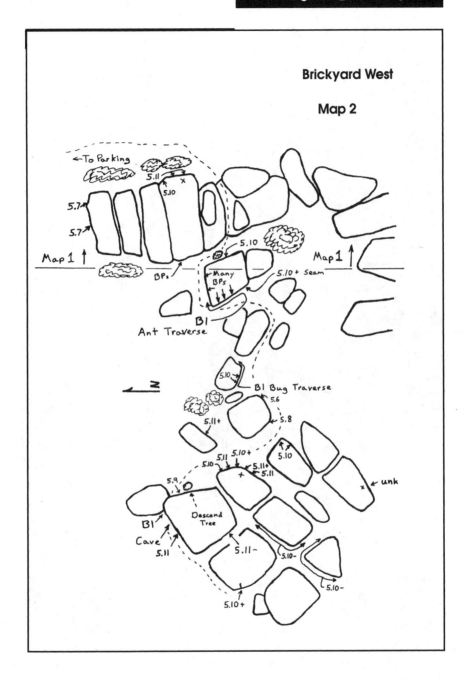

Brickyard West

Map 2

*John Perlin using the "Brickyard Technique" for the tricky summit moves on
"The Prow" (5.11-) at the Brickyard.*

PAINTED CAVE

Painted Cave is the most popular natural rock bouldering area near Santa Barbara. Easy access makes this a great place for locals—or anyone travelling Highway 101—to get a quick workout. The rock is soft, overhanging sandstone with numerous flakes and finger pockets. The two large boulders are riddled with quality problems and traverses. **Heavy Traffic** is usually top-roped or one can jump off after grabbing the jugs to avoid the 5.11 finish. A third boulder 50 feet down the road (south) has a good traverse and several short problems.

The boulder field just before Painted Cave is on private property and is off limits to climbers. Poison oak is abundant. The season is year-round, except after rain. Avoid all sandstone climbing when the rock is wet. Many good holds have broken off when climbers used them before the rock has had a chance to dry, often making the route unclimbable.

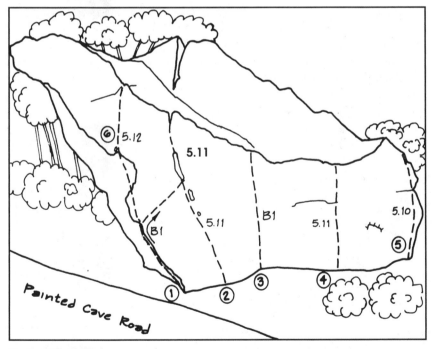

Trojan Boulder

1. **Steps Ahead B1**
   Overhanging start to traverse.
2. **Heavy Traffic 5.11** TR
3. **Big Deal B1**

4. **The Old Soft Hsu 5.11**
5. **Arête 5.10-**
6. **Trojan War 5.12** TR
6a. **Sit-down start B1+**

Roof Boulder
1. **The Wedgie Roof B2**

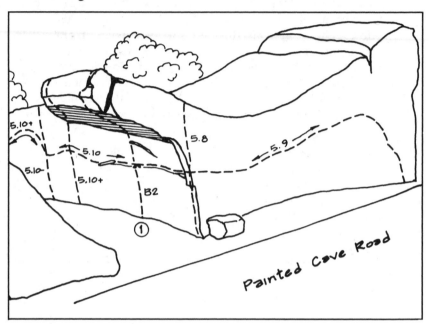

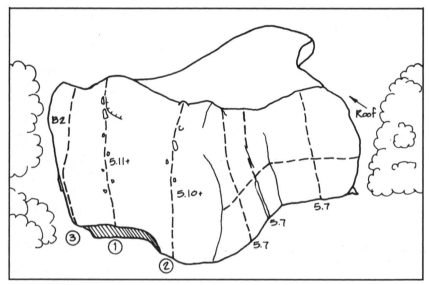

Lower Roof Boulder
1. **Static Eliminator 5.11+ ★** Pockets.
2. **The Baby's Head 5.10+ ★**
3. **Flake Problem B2/B2+**

PATTERSON WALL

This artificial wall is very popular with Santa Barbara students and
locals. The climbing is on a railroad bridge crossing the Maria
Ygnacio Creek and is accessed by the bike trail. The holds are formed
by natural irregularities in the blocks which give the impression of
climbing on natural rock. Most climbers get a quick forearm pump
working on the traverses of each wall. Also, there are numerous
routes which go straight up, are 5.8-5.11, and can easily be top-roped.

Patterson Wall Road Map

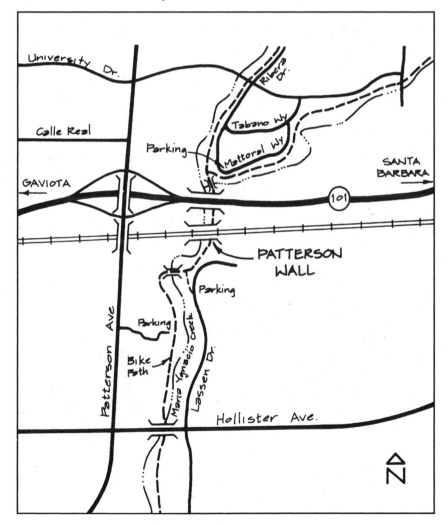

There are six bouldering areas in Ventura County: **The Swimming Hole, Ojai Area, Camarillo Grove Boulder, Coyote Beach, The Gainsborough Boulder** and **Point Mugu**. Each area is unique and receives a detailed description in the following sections.

Ventura County Area

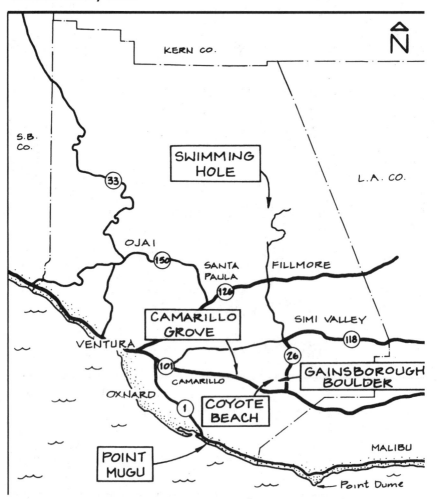

THE SWIMMING HOLE

The Swimming Hole is a newly developed bouldering area located in the Sespe Condor Sanctuary. The sandstone boulders and short walls line a lush stream bed in a true wilderness setting. This area is only recommended to expert boulderers accompanied by a set of expert spotters. The majority of problems are very difficult with poor landings. The remoteness of the area tends to make the boulders look even more difficult. A twisted ankle could turn the hike into a major epic and a solo boulderer with a serious injury might not be found for weeks.

This area was developed in the late eighties and early nineties, with Paul Anderson and Jeff Johnson being largely responsible for many of the classic hard problems. The Swimming Hole can be climbed all year, but avoid hot days, high water (spring run-off) and days after rain. Poison oak is abundant and bugs can be numerous at times. There is unlimited access at this time, but that may change if condors are reintroduced to the area.

Paul Anderson climbing "Pocket Change" (B1), Swimming Hole.

Photo by Damian Gebert.

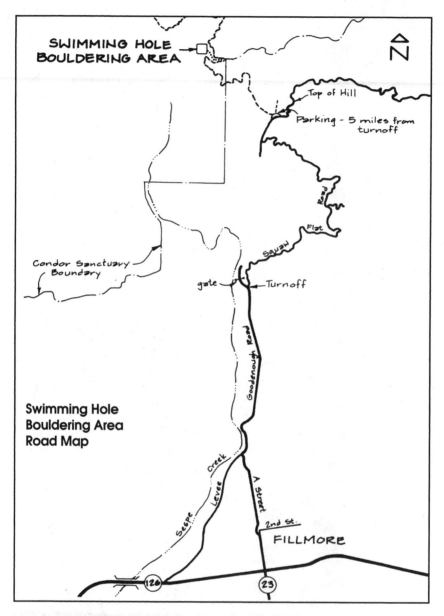

SWIMMING HOLE
BOULDERING AREA

N

Top of Hill

Parking - 5 miles from turnoff

Road

Flat

Squaw

Condor Sanctuary
Boundary

gate — Turnoff

Goodenough Road

**Swimming Hole
Bouldering Area
Road Map**

Creek

Levee

A Street

2nd St.
FILLMORE

Sespe

126

23

Directions:
Take the 126 to Fillmore. Turn north at the 23 (A Street) in downtown Fillmore. Make a right onto Goodenough Road and continue up until a turnoff with a sign for Oak Flat Station and Dough Flat. Set your mileage gauge to zero at the junction and proceed up the narrow, mostly paved road for almost five miles. Park at a large turnoff on the left. Take the lefthand trail, uphill past an iron gate, then downhill for approximately 45 minutes to a streambed. Boulder hop downstream for about 10 minutes to the first boulders. Boulders can be found for another quarter of a mile. Allow an hour or longer to hike back out.

Dimitri Fritz on Raindance, at Swimming Hole.
Photo by Damian Gebert.

OJAI AREAS:

THE FOOT

To reach **The Foot**, drive past numerous private properties and no trespassing signs until you reach the National Forest access. Do not park
where traffic could be impeded (approaching via mountain bike will
alleviate potential hassles). A relatively low-angle sandstone bluff
will be found 100 yards up the Foothill Trail. Numerous cracks and
bolted faces have been done on this small face. Bouldering can also
be found up the Foothill Trail. Be careful of abundant poison oak.

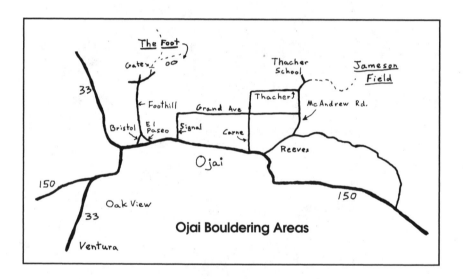

Ojai Bouldering Areas

JAMESON FIELD

Sparse bouldering can be found at **Jameson Field** and in the surrounding environs. Drive to Thacher School and turn right at the entrance.
Follow signs to Jameson Field and Park. The school allows climbing,
but discourages the use of chalk on the boulders.

CAMARILLO GROVE BOULDER

This lonely cube is worth checking out for a quick bouldering session.
It's right off Highway 101. A $3.00 fee is charged to park inside the
County Park. Interestingly enough, the boulder rolled down the hill
from the crags above 101 to its present location. The rock is volcanic
breccia and is rife with steep pocketed face climbs. The season is
year-round and poison oak is abundant. This boulder is on private
property and access is sometimes questionable. Check with park
headquarters on access information.

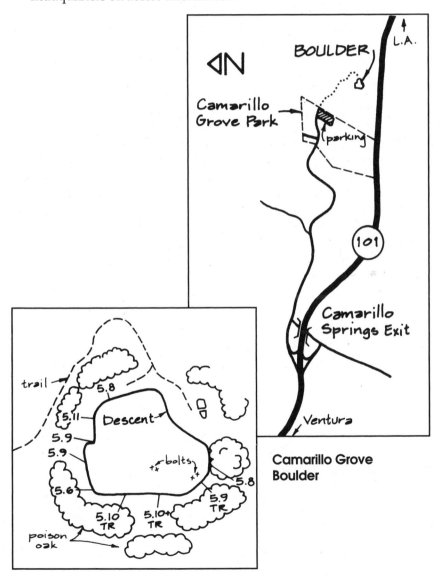

Camarillo Grove Boulder

COYOTE BEACH

Coyote Beach is a recently discovered and undeveloped area in
Newbury Park. The rock is generally very soft, but in places where it
has been water polished, good bouldering can be found. The main
climbing area straddles a stream, with steep sandstone walls on both
sides of the canyon between two small waterfalls. The northeast wall
of the canyon has a long overhanging traverse and a few short steep
problems with sloping mantle finishes. On the overhanging and
pocketed southwest wall there are several hard-looking problems,
probably in the 5.10 to 5.12 range. A large boulder in the middle of
the stream that creates the southern-most waterfall looks as if it may
also have a few routes. The rock here is hard, but needs cleaning
since the area has seen very little climbing. Further downstream at a
bend in the stream is a short bolted roof problem climbing out of a
low cave. The cave also sports a good pumpy traverse.

To get to Coyote Beach, take Highway 101 to Newbury Park and exit at
Ventu Park Road. Go north to the intersection with Hillcrest Drive
and park. Continue walking north about 200 yards along Ventu Park
until you come to a dirt road on the right. This road turns into a trail
which winds along the canyon next to the stream. A 10 minute walk
will get you to the main area. The poison oak-lined trail takes you
above the bouldering on the northwest side, so you must drop down
and backtrack just past the second waterfall. Coyote Park is located
within a State Nature Preserve and access is questionable. Tread
lightly and pick up all trash you see lying around.

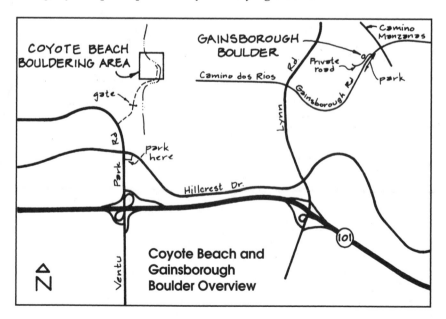

Coyote Beach and Gainsborough Boulder Overview

GAINSBOROUGH BOULDER

From Lynn Road, travel east about a half mile on Gainsborough Road to a small pile of boulders on the lower flanks of the hillside to the left of the road. Two or three difficult, off-the-deck problems can be found on the prominent overhanging sandstone boulder. A bolted top-rope anchor is available for the squeamish.

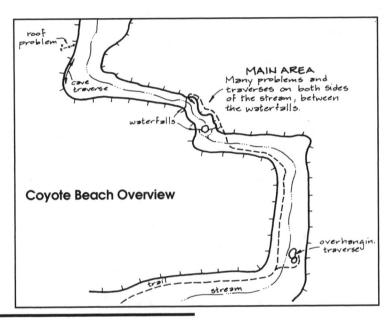

POINT MUGU

Point Mugu is a popular area for locals and travelers along the coast route (Highway 1). The sandstone wall is slightly overhanging and is split by many cracks and features. The routes are usually bouldered, but beginners may opt for a top-rope. Several climbs exist on the formation west of the boulder, including a classic dihedral lieback 5.8 lead route.

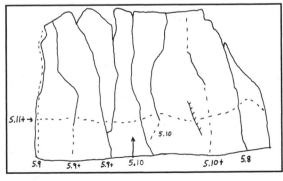

**Point Mugu Overview
Directions:** The graffiti-covered boulder is very obvious from the Pacific Coast Highway. It sits just off the road in a large parking area along the beach side of the PCH just south of the Point.

Los Angeles County, with its vast metropolitan sprawl, is also the unlikely home of vast amounts of rock. The northwestern hills include the Santa Monica and Santa Susana Mountains, which are covered with many untouched volcanic and sandstone boulderfields. Much of the rock is of poor quality, but new areas with excellent rock are being uncovered frequently.

The San Gabriel Mountains are composed of granitic rock and have miles of untapped potential as well. The only popular bouldering areas are **Horse Flats** and **Mt. Baldy**.

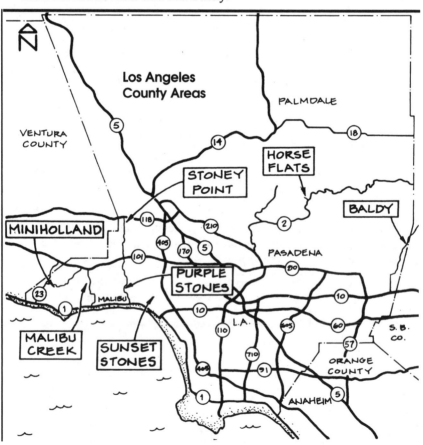

MINIHOLLAND BOULDERING AREA

This first-rate but limited bouldering area is located on Mulholland Highway between Highway 23 and Kanan Road 0.9 miles east of Highway 23. From The Pacific Coast Highway, drive north on Decker Canyon Road and turn right on Mulholland. From Highway 101, drive south on Westlake Boulevard and turn left on Mulholland, and drive until you see the boulders on the right side of the road.

The rock is volcanic breccia of the same type found at Malibu Creek State Park and it provides excellent steep-pocketed face climbs and difficult overhanging traverses. You will find the best climbing on Boulders 1 and 2, but may wish to make the five-minute bushwack down to Boulder 4 if you are in search of more overhanging rock.

Miniholland Road Map

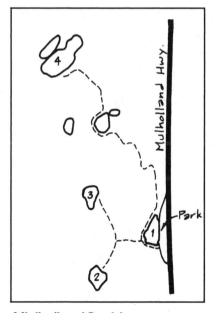

Miniholland Boulders

MALIBU CREEK

Malibu Creek consists of two separate areas, **Malibu Creek State Park** and **Malibu Creek Tunnel**. The Malibu Creek Tunnel bouldering is on sandstone, similar to Stoney Point, but these river boulders have undergone severe weathering and water polishing, resulting in a very solid, high-quality rock.

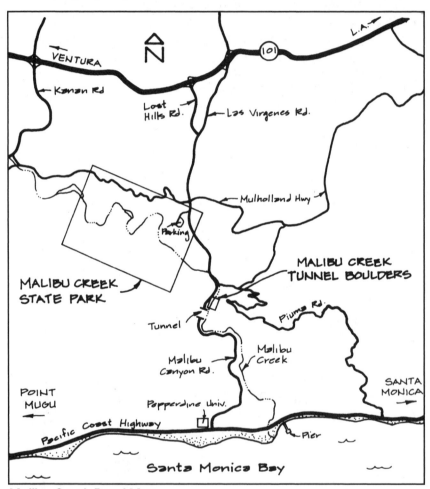

Malibu Creek Road Map

Directions to Malibu Creek State Park:

Take Las Virgenes south from Highway 101 on the Malibu Canyon Road north from the Pacific Coast Highway. The entrance to the park, on the west side of the road, is well marked. Parking for the Malibu Tunnel area is located about 1.5 miles south of the park entrance and a quarter mile north of the tunnel. There is a large trailhead parking area here. Walk south along the road a short distance to the first large roadcut on the canyon (east) side of the road. A trail leads into the canyon from here.

The tunnel rock was the first of the two Malibu areas to be discovered with bouldering potential, but soon fell out of popularity with the discovery of the climbing in Malibu State Park. In the early eighties, Mike Guardino began to develop the climbing in the State Park, calling it "Little Europe." The area was slow to gain popularity due to lack of good information and propagated rumors of poor quality rock. Still, a small contingent of locals, knowing the true quality of the climbing and reveling in the lack of other climbers, slowly developed the area. Bill Levanthal, Mike Guardino and Matt Dancy were the most active in this early exploration. Since the last edition of this guide, bouldering development of the rock pool area has greatly increased, transforming the rock pool area into possibly the finest bouldering in Southern California for the expert boulderer. The pocketed rock is a volcanic breccia and quality boulder problems and traverses are abundant. The cave is the gem of the area. The 20- to 30-foot, 60 degree overhanging wall with spaced pockets has some of the most extreme bouldering in Southern California. Paul Anderson and Jeff Johnson were largely responsible for the cave's development. The ratings given on the cave traverse are for completing the entire traverse.

The bouldering here appeals more to the expert climber because of the degree of difficulty (mostly 5.10 and up) and rarely offers decent landing areas. The climber must be well versed at reversing sections rather than taking an uncontrolled fall into shallow water or onto rock-strewn bases. Just getting into the canyon may be more of a challenge than beginning climbers are ready to handle.

The climbing on the **Ghetto Wall** and **The Planet of the Apes** wall has also become very popular with sport climbers. The **Ghetto Wall** offers sport climbing leads on overhanging pocketed rock and is shady most of the time. During high water, access is very difficult. The **Planet of the Apes** wall is mostly top-rope routes and faces south. It bakes in the summer, but is very nice in the cooler months and is so overhanging that you can do the bouldering traverse in a rain storm.

A fee of $5.00 is required for parking inside Malibu Creek State Park and the park closes at sunset. A no bolting rule was enforced by the rangers a few years ago, but new bolts continue to appear with no action taken against them. Poison oak and stinging nettle are found in abundance.

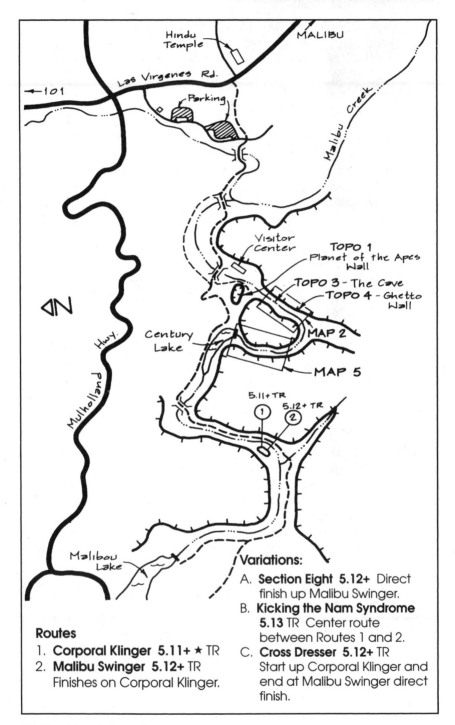

Routes

1. **Corporal Klinger 5.11+ ★** TR
2. **Malibu Swinger 5.12+** TR
   Finishes on Corporal Klinger.

Variations:

A. **Section Eight 5.12+** Direct finish up Malibu Swinger.
B. **Kicking the Nam Syndrome 5.13** TR Center route between Routes 1 and 2.
C. **Cross Dresser 5.12+** TR Start up Corporal Klinger and end at Malibu Swinger direct finish.

Malibu Creek Overview

Jeff Johnson on the 5.10 problem above "The Cave" at Malibu Creek. Photo by Damian Gebert.

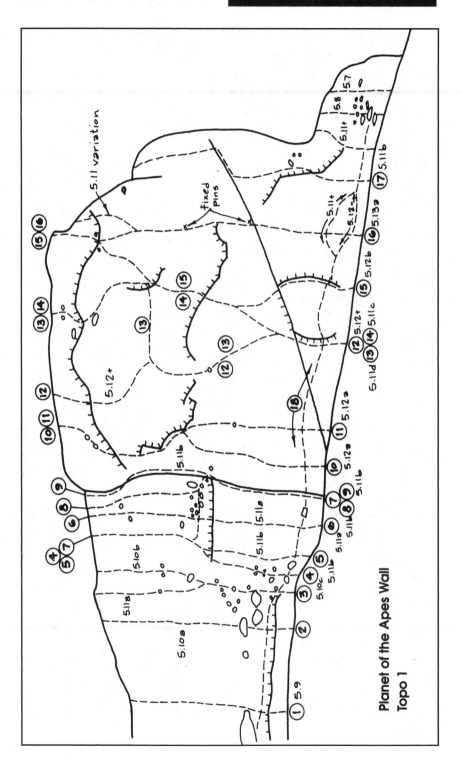

Planet of the Apes Wall
Topo 1

Malibu Creek
Planet of the Apes Wall
Topo 1
1. **Grape Ape 5.9** TR
2. **Christmas Pump 5.10a** TR
3. **Shock the Monkey 5.10 b- 5.11a** TR
4. **Spiker Monkey 5.10c** TR
5. **Spider Monkey 5.11b ★** TR
6. **Finger Prints 5.11a** TR
7. **Planet of the Apes 5.11a ★** TR
8. **Birthday Boy 5.11b ★** TR
9. **The Crack 5.11b** TR
10. **Gorilla of My Dreams 5.12a** TR
11. **Gorilla Warfare 5.12a** TR
12. **Apes of Wrath 5.12+** TR
13. **Spank the Monkey 5.11d** TR
14. **Monkey Sang, Monkey Do 5.11c** TR
15. **Monkey Business 5.12b** TR
16. **Simian Survival 5.13a** TR
17. **Walking on the Moon 5.11b** TR
18. **Planet of the Apes Traverse B1 ★** Rating
    for completion of entire length.

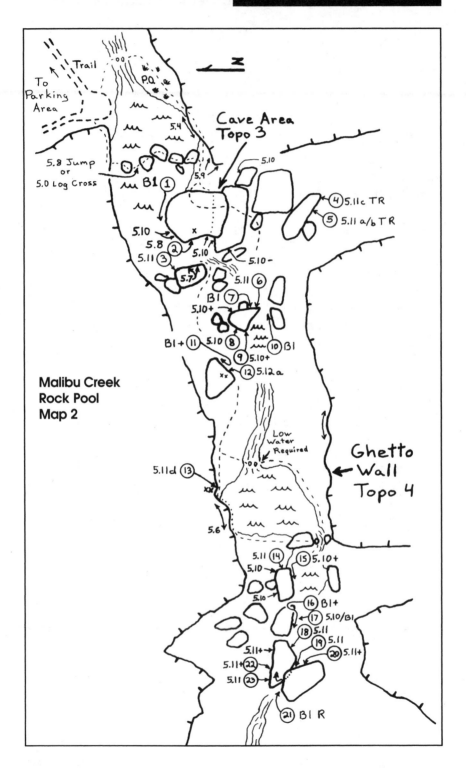

Malibu Creek Rock Pool
Map 2

1. **Anderson Traverse B1** Traverse over water.
2. **Classic Malibu Face 5.8** ★ TR
3. **Gutterball 5.11**
4. **Nipple Denial Syndrome 5.11c** TR Rope toss to sling tree for TR.
5. **Letter Box 5.11a/b** TR
6. **Niagara Fist 5.11** ★ R
7. **Anderson Problem B1** R
8. **The Lunker 5.10** ★ Traverse over water to start.
9. **Black Box 5.10+** Very low water required.
10. **Kaptain Traverse B1**
11. **Evenflow B1+**
12. **Hot Lips 5.12** ★ TR
13. **Beast of the East 5.11d** TR
14. **Water Hazard 5.11** ★
15. **Traverse or Submerse 5.10+**
16. **Kerwin Problem B1+** Start low in alcove on right side. The traverse from left to right is B1-.
17. **Pocketed Wall 5.10/B1** Many variations.
18. **Dead Finger 5.11**
19. **Crank Session or Swim Lessons 5.11** ★ Traverse from right to left above log.
20. **Swim Wear 5.11+** R
20a. **Bridge over Troubled Waters 5.11-** Use back wall as chimney.
21. **Lunge or Plunge B1** ★ R
22. **Power Beast 5.11+** R
23. **Celluloid Hero 5.11** R

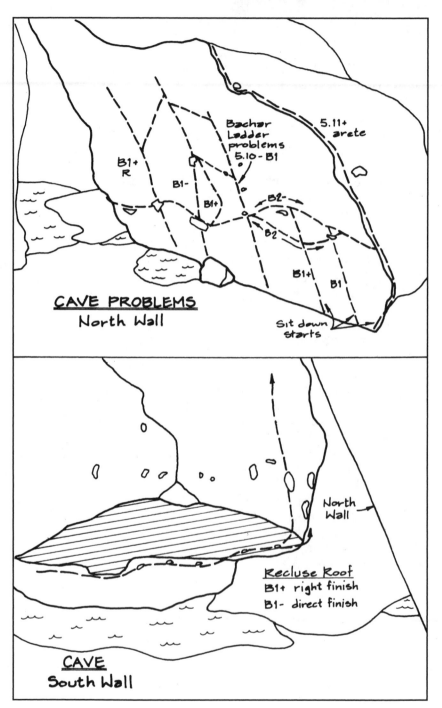

Malibu Creek Topo 3, Cave Area

Ghetto Wall Topo 4 (Lead Routes)

1. The Projects 5.13a
2. Skeezer Pleaser 5.11c ★
3. Kathmandu 5.10a
4. Stun Gun 5.12c/d ★
4a. Stunning Gun 5.13a Direct start, clip first bolt on Stun Gun.

5. Maximum Ghetto 5.13a ★
6. Darkest Hour 5.12c ★
7. Johnny Can't Lead 5.10d ★
8. Hole Patrol 5.12a/b
9. Stink Finger 5.12c
10. Urban Struggle 5.12 a ★

11. Suburban Struggle 5.11b R
12. Toxeth Walk 5.12c
13. Junk Ramp 5.9
14. Dead Rats 5.9 Around corner from route 13.

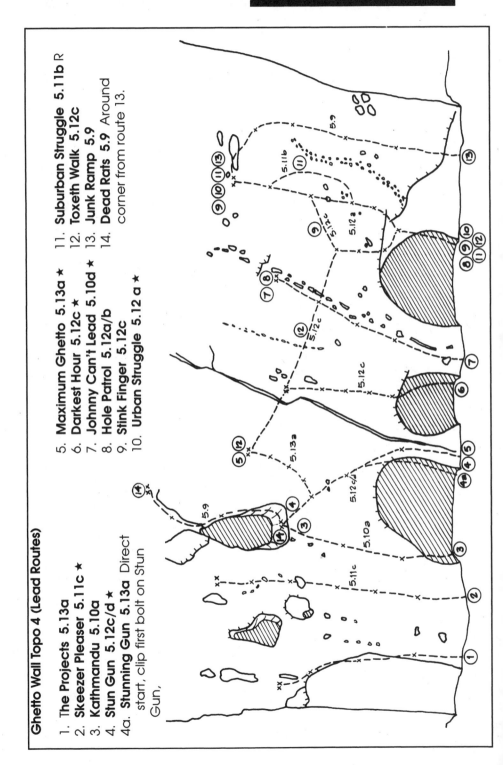

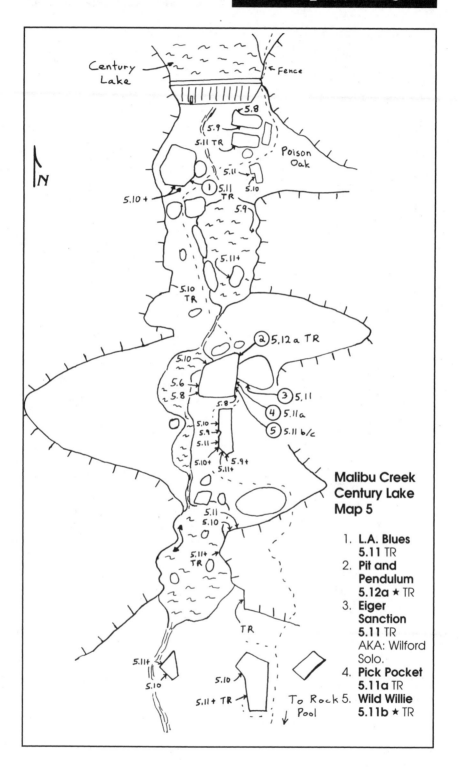

Century Lake

← Fence

5.8

5.9

5.11 TR

Poison Oak

5.11

5.11 TR 5.10

5.10 +

① 5.11 TR

5.9

5.11+

5.10 TR

② 5.12 a TR

5.10

5.6 5.8

③ 5.11

5.8

④ 5.11a

5.10

5.9

5.11

⑤ 5.11 b/c

5.10+ 5.9+

5.11+

5.11 5.10

5.11+ TR

Malibu Creek Century Lake Map 5

5.11+

5.10

TR

5.11+

5.10

5.10

5.11+ TR

To Rock Pool

1. **L.A. Blues 5.11** TR
2. **Pit and Pendulum 5.12a** ★ TR
3. **Eiger Sanction 5.11** TR
   AKA: Wilford Solo.
4. **Pick Pocket 5.11a** TR
5. **Wild Willie 5.11b** ★ TR

Dimitri Fritz on the pocketed "Gutter Ball" (5.11), Malibu Creek State Park.

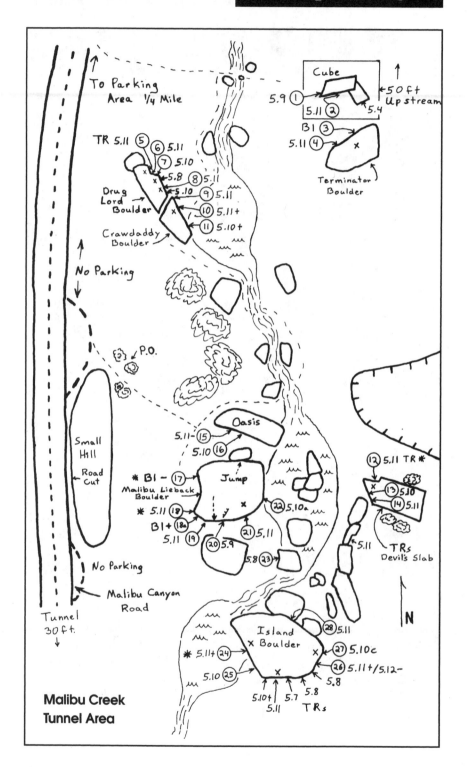

To Parking
Area ¼ Mile

Cube

5.9 ①
5.11 ②   5.4
←50ft
Up stream

B1 ③
5.11 ④   X

Terminator
Boulder

TR 5.11 ⑤
⑥ 5.11
⑦ 5.10
X
Drug   X   5.8 ⑧ 5.11
Lord   X   5.10 ⑨ 5.11
Boulder   X ⑩ 5.11+
Crawdaddy   ⑪ 5.10+
Boulder

No Parking

P.O.

Small
Hill

Road
Cut

Oasis

5.11– ⑮
5.10 ⑯

* B1 – ⑰   Jump
Malibu Lieback
Boulder

* 5.11 ⑱   X

B1+ ⑱ₐ
5.11 ⑲   ② 5.9
           ㉑ 5.11
           5.8 ㉓

㉒ 5.10a

⑫ 5.11 TR *
X ㉓
⑬ 5.10
⑭ 5.11

5.11

TRs
Devil's Slab

No Parking

Malibu Canyon
Road

Tunnel
30 ft.
↓

㉘ 5.11
Island
X Boulder   ㉗ 5.10c

* 5.11+ ㉔   X   ㉖ 5.11+/5.12–
5.10 ㉕   X   5.8
           5.10+ 5.7 5.8
           5.11   TRs

N

**Malibu Creek
Tunnel Area**

Malibu Creek Tunnel Area

1. **Blockhead 5.9** Mantel.
2. **Powder Edge 5.11** ★ Traverse from corner.
3. **Terminator B1**
4. **Procrastinator 5.11**
5. **Kingpin Variation 5.11** TR
6. **Drug Load 5.11**
7. **Buzz Saw 5.10**
8. **Redstone 5.11** TR
9. **Flyweenakiss 5.11+** TR
10. **Crawdaddy 5.11+** TR
11. **Flydaddy 5.10+**
12. **El Diablo 5.11** ★ TR
13. **Lycra Boy 5.10** Brown stain.
14. **Lycra Man 5.11**
15. **Oasis 5.11-**
16. **Bouldering for Dollars 5.10**
17. **Overlord B1-** ★
18. **The Prow 5.11** ★
18a.**Avalon B1+** ★
19. **Crocodile Rock 5.11**
20. **Malibu Lieback 5.9**
21. **Giant Steps Unfold 5.11b/c**
22. **Department of Water and Power 5.10**
23. **Test Tube 5.8**
24. **Islands in the Stream 5.11+** ★ Roof.
25. **Luckyman 5.10** Overhang.
26. **Trash Compactor 5.11+/5.12-** TR
27. **Apparatus 5.10** ★

PURPLE STONES

The **Purple Stones** is a small bouldering area located just downstream from the town of Topanga. The area lies in a deep canyon, with a quiet stream and thick riparian forest. The rock is a very solid, richly-colored sandstone, with bands of polished pebbles and pockets formed by anti-pebbles. The climbing is bold in general, with landings on jumbled rocks or in shallow water. A top-rope is recommended for most problems, though some locals seem to have no need for one.

Banny Root (Jim May) and Dave Katz discovered the area in the mid-seventies and, with the help of Bob Gaines, Robert Carrere, Dan Scdoris, Mark Bowling, and others, developed the area through the early eighties. Bill Levanthal also had a hand in this development and created many of the classic very hard problems such as **Ultraviolet** and **Men at Sea**. Originally, the boulders had a soft sand base, and the stream took a completely different course than it does now. Each year, the winter rains change the area; someday maybe the sand will be back. The season is year-round, except after heavy rains.

The parking spot shown on the map is technically illegal, but there is no sign at that spot and climbers have rarely been ticketed or hassled

here. If you want to feel 100% safe, park at Cal Gas and walk down the road. Transients and partiers often frequent the area, leaving trash and graffiti behind. The area was a popular spot for hippies and bikers during the sixties and seventies and was referred to as "Twin Pools."

Bill Leventhal about to get high above the pond on "Pebble Beach" (5.11), Purple Stones.

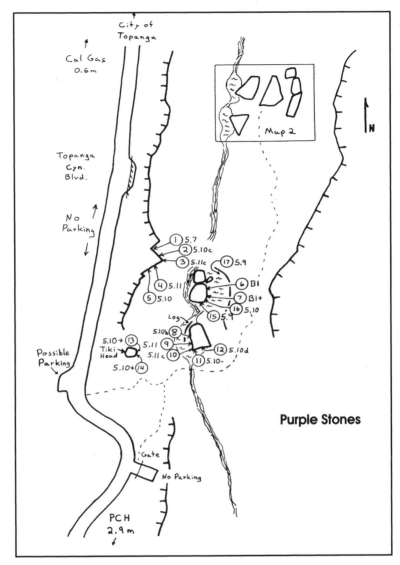

Purple Stones South

1. **Barney Rubble 5.7** Lead.
2. **Pebbles and Bam Bam 5.10c** TR
3. **The Color Purple 5.11c** TR
4. **Flintlock 5.11** ★ TR
5. **Betty Rubble 5.10** TR
6. **Asteroid Belt B1** R
7. **Chicken Cacciatore B1+** R
   Avoid arête.
8. **Mantel Core 5.10 b**
9. **Take a Pebble 5.10c**
10. **The Water's Edge Left 5.11c**
11. **The Water's Edge Right 5.10-** ★
12. **The Water Strider 5.10d** ★
13. **Macadamia Nut 5.10+**
14. **Hawaiian Host 5.10+**
15. **Poprocks 5.9** ★
16. **Pebble Crack 5.10**
17. **Traverse 5.9**

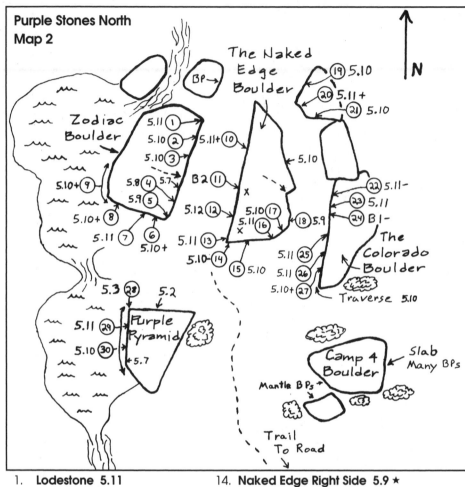

Purple Stones North
Map 2

1. **Lodestone 5.11**
2. **Muscle Beach 5.10**
3. **Nude Beach; Left 5.10, Right 5.10+**
4. **Sandy Beach 5.8**
5. **Pebble Arête 5.9**
6. **Pebble Direct 5.10+** ★
7. **Zodiac Direct 5.11** ★
8. **Hallucination 5.10+**
9. **Zodiac Traverse 5.10+**
10. **Purple Haze 5.11+** ★
11. **Ultraviolet B2**
12. **Atlantis 5.12a** ★ TR Traverse to Ultraviolet at mid-height.
12a. **Men at Sea 5.12c** TR Direct finish.
12b. **Triple Direct B1** Traverse to Naked Edge.
13. **Naked Edge 5.11** ★
14. **Naked Edge Right Side 5.9** ★
15. **Undercling Direct 5.10** TR
16. **Rastafarian 5.11** TR
17. **Purple Seedless 5.10c**
18. **Steppin Stone 5.9+**
19. **Hawaiian Face 5.10**
20. **Katsy Corner 5.11** ★ AKA: Pungi Sticks.
21. **Pungi Face 5.10**
22. **Pan Am 5.11-**
23. **Key Largo 5.11**
24. **Corkscrew B1**
25. **Large Kilo 5.11**
26. **Launch Ledge 5.11**
27. **Free Bird 5.10+**
28. **Pyramid Arête 5.3** ★ Goes no-hands.
29. **Pebble Beach 5.11** ★
30. **Topanga Lieback 5.10**

SUNSET STONES

This remote and scenic sandstone bouldering area is set in the hills
above Pacific Palisades. **Sunset Stones** was originally developed in
the late seventies and early eighties by a group of local climbers led
by David Katz, Bob Gaines and Banny Root. Initial development fol-
lowed a brush fire, which cleared most of the vegetation and allowed
easy access to the rocks. Currently, the area is very overgrown and
looks like it hasn't seen much climbing in recent years. The rock is
good quality sandstone, similar to what you'll find at Stoney Point,
with abundant flakes and pockets. A renaissance in climbing here
would likely result in many new routes and variations, particularly
on **Mega Boulder** and **Skull Rock**.

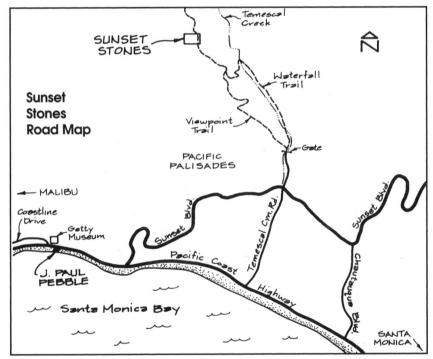

Directions: Follow Temescal Canyon Road to its end just north of Sunset
Boulevard and park next to the trailhead in the Presbyterian Conference
Center lot. Skirting the conference center grounds, the trail follows the west
side of Temescal Creek and crosses to the east just past the second of two
debris basins about five minutes up the canyon. Recross the creek at 1.3 miles
near a small waterfall and follow the steepening trail up switchbacks to the
ridge crest. Continue another five minutes along the ridge crest and the prominent Skull Rock will become visible on your left. This very scenic hike is 2.1
miles one way and takes about 40 minutes. A good variation on a clear day is
to return to the parking lot via the Viewpoint Trail, which offers beautiful
panoramic coastal views. Bicycles are not allowed on the trails.

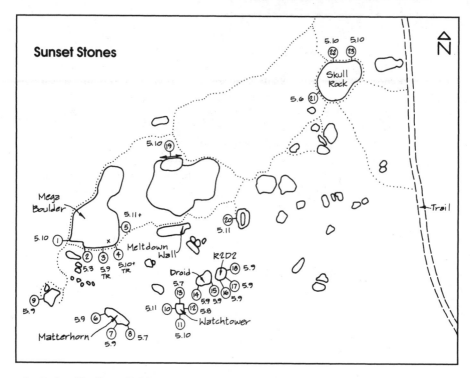

1. **Bobs Big Boy 5.10**
   Overhanging crack.
2. **Ramp 5.3 ★**
3. **Hunks of Chunks 5.9 TR**
   Loose. Bolt needs hanger.
4. **Molarity of the Polarity
   5.10+TR*** Bolt needs hanger.
5. **Powderfinger 5.11+**
6. **North Face 5.9 ★**
7. **Pumping Sandstone 5.9**
8. **Sanctuary 5.7**
9. **Bowls of Holes 5.9**
10. **Thief 5.11 ★**
11. **Joker 5.10**
12. **Barefoot Servant 5.8**
13. **Princess 5.7**
14. **Master Cylinder 5.9**
15. **The Droid's Roids 5.9**
16. **Wookie 5.9**
17. **Battlestar 5.9**
18. **Lorne Green 5.9**
19. **Gunsmoke Traverse 5.10 ★**
20. **Toad's Lip Mantel 5.11**
21. **Downclimb 5.6**
22. **Giant Step 5.10 ★**
23. **Treasure Island 5.10**

THE J. PAUL PEBBLE

This huge beachside pebble has some boulder and top-roping possibilities. In an article in a past *Climbing* magazine, John Long described the history and assets of this boulder; but far better alternatives are found a quick drive north to **Malibu Creek** or **Purple Stones**. If you're already at the beach, however, the Pebble may provide some entertainment. The rock is a conglomerate sandstone.

STONEY POINT

Stoney Point is a Chatsworth city park in the San Fernando Valley. The area is actually a large hill with steep walls on several of its sides, with large, quality boulders strewn all around the base. The walls provide many great top-rope and lead routes, but Stoney Point is mainly known as a bouldering area and is perhaps the most popular in Southern California. Though hundreds of boulders and faces exist here, it seems that most people prefer to climb on Boulder One, Turlock Boulder, and B1 Boulder. Hundreds of problems and variations exist on these three boulders. Therefore, there is no way to document them all in this guidebook, so only the most obvious distinct lines and problems are shown.

The rock is a soft sandstone with flakes, pockets and a few cracks. Like all sandstone areas, the rock is especially subject to failure when wet. Please allow the rock to thoroughly dry after a rain to prevent key holds from breaking off.

Aside from being an excellent bouldering area, Stoney's primary attraction seems to be the social scene. When the days are long, groups of locals can be found every evening on some desperate variation or new problem. The groups, providing spots and taking turns working out the sequences, push each other to the limit of bouldering excellence.

Mike Waugh on "Boulder One" at Stoney Point. Photo by Kevin Powell.

The history of Stoney Point goes back to the very beginning of climbing in California. Glen Dawson and other Sierra Club mountaineers first began climbing at Stoney around 1935. After World War II, climbing increased rapidly here, and in the early fifties Stoney became the training ground for Royal Robbins, Yvon Chouinard, Chuck Wilts, TM Herbert, Tom Frost, Bob Kamps, and a host of others who were to later usher in the modern climbing at Tahquitz Rock and Yosemite. These climbers developed many of the standard problems up to 5.11, but always considered bouldering as merely training for "real" rock climbing. Not until the seventies did bouldering-for-its-own-sake gain popularity. John Bachar, John Long, Mike Waugh, Dean Fidelman and the ever-present Kamps were some of the early boulderers developing Stoney's hard modern circuit. Paul Neil, Mike Pope, Chris Wegener and Jim Wilson were also especially active during this period, and pioneered many of the backside areas and numerous top-rope problems. The eighties brought various new contributors to Stoney's development. Bill Levanthal and Matt Oliphant worked on the backside and surrounding areas, finding many new problems. Later in the eighties, Paul Anderson and Jeff Johnson were responsible for continuing new finds, as were long-time activists Waugh, Kamps, Rich Lake, and Herb Laeger.

Stoney Point is a city park and access for climbing is unlimited. However, its proximity to a metropolitan area makes it subject to severe overcrowding and abuse. Graffiti, trash, and broken glass are all prevalent. As well as these unnatural hazards, poison oak is found on the backside, summit area, and at the north end. The season extends year-round, although in summer, the evening is the best time to avoid the heat.

Stoney Point Overview Map Key

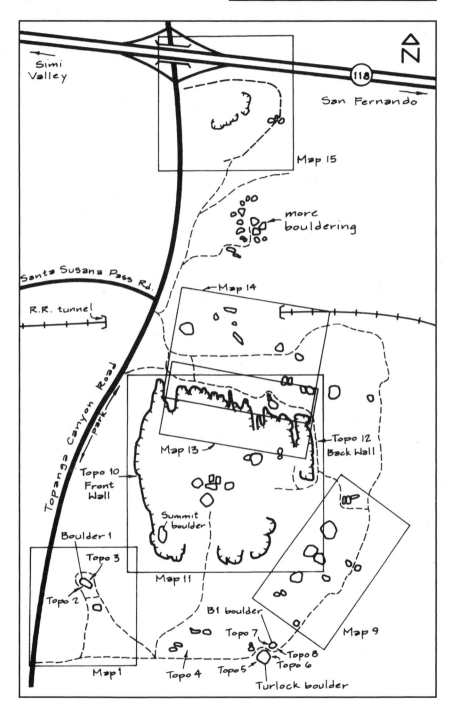

Simi Valley

San Fernando

118

N

Map 15

more bouldering

Santa Susana Pass Rd.

R.R. tunnel

Map 14

Topo 12 Back Wall

Map 13

Topanga Canyon Road

Park

Topo 10 Front Wall

Summit boulder

Map 11

Boulder 1

Topo 3

Topo 2

B1 boulder

Topo 7

Topo 8
Topo 6

Map 9

Map 1

Topo 4

Topo 5

Turlock boulder

Stoney Point Overview

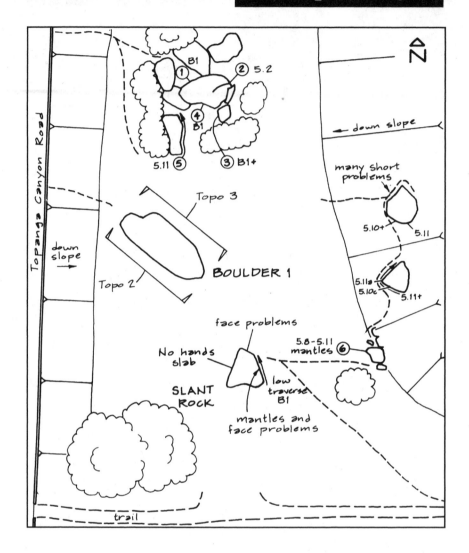

Parking Lot Area
Map 1

1. **Crank Queenie B1 R ★** Many variations.
2. **Jam Crack 5.2**
3. **Say Goodnight B1+** No right arête.
4. **Aftershock B1**
5. **Pump Traverse 5.11** With no lip holds, B1.
6. **Wilson's Mantels 5.8-5.11** Many variations.

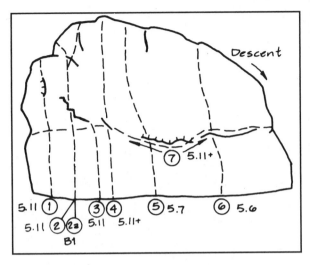

Boulder One, South Face
Topo 2

1. **Nylon Boy 5.11**
2. **Boot Flake Direct 5.11**
2a. **Double Dyno B1** Dyno variation.
3. **Boot Flake 5.11 ★** Many variations.
4. **Endo Boy 5.11+ ★**
5. **Short Story 5.7 ★**
6. **Vivarin 5.6 ★**

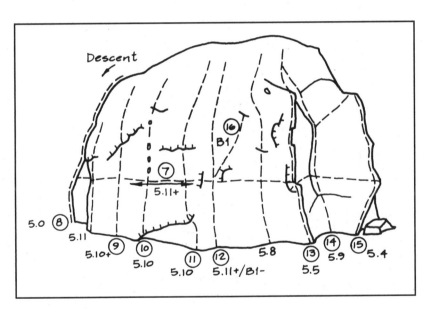

Boulder One, North Face
Topo 3

7. **Traverse of Boulder One 5.11+**
8. **Descent Route 5.0**
9. **"WD-40" 5.10+**
10. **Three Pigs 5.10** Chiseled holds.
11. **Undercling 5.10**
11a. **Yabo Mantel B1-** Avoid the chopped hold.

12. **Vaino's Dyno 5.11+/B1-**
13. **The Nose 5.5 ★**
14. **Dihedral Left 5.9**
14a. **Dihedral Right 5.10c**
15. **The Arête 5.4**
16. **Leaping Lizards B1** Full flying dyno.

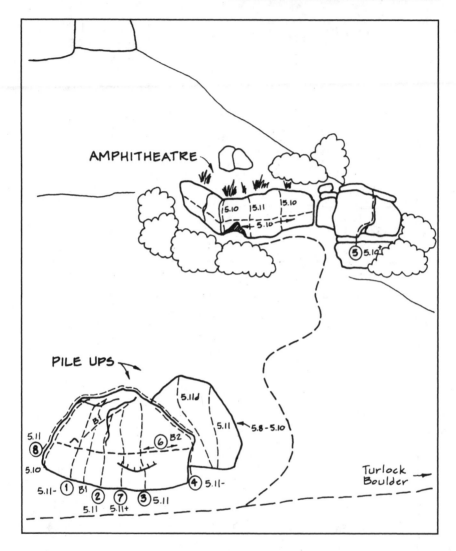

Pile Ups and Amphitheatre
Topo 4
1. **Pile Driver 5.11-** ★
2. **Pile Lieback 5.11**
3. **Sledgehammer 5.11**
4. **Pile Up Mantel 5.11-**
5. **Black Roof 5.10+** TR
6. **Anderson Traverse B2**
7. **Gomer Pile 5.11+** Sit down start in undercling.
8. **Pile Ups Lip Traverse 5.11**

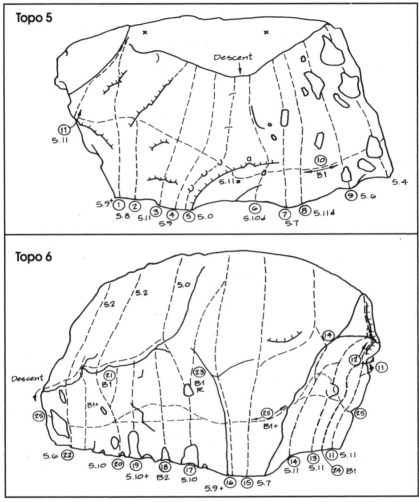

Turlock Boulder, West & South Faces
Topo 5
1. **Silent running 5.9+**
2. **The Flake 5.8**
3. **Eliminate Face 5.11**
4. **Turlock Face 5.9**
5. **Carved Holds 5.0** Descent route.
6. **The Bulge 5.10 d**
7. **Untold Story 5.7**
8. **Point Blank 5.11d** Broken hold.
9. **Potholes 5.6** Many variations.
10. **Traverse of Turlock B1**
11. **The Corner 5.11**

Turlock Boulder, North & East Faces
Topo 6
11. **The Corner 5.11 ★**

12. **Turlock Crack 5.11+** OTD
13. **Crystal Ball 5.11** OTD
14. **Crowd Pleaser 5.11 ★** OTD
15. **North Face 5.7** Many variations.
16. **North Face Arête 5.9+**
17. **Hoof and Mouth 5.10 ★**
18. **Waugh Problem B2**
19. **Slime 5.10 + ★** Many variations.
20. **Pliers 5.10 ★** Many variations.
21. **The Real Crystal Ball Mantle B1**
22. **Ramada 5.6**
23. **Nose Dive B1** R Avoid chiseled hold.
24. **Waugh Problem II B1**
25. **Turlock Low Traverse B1+**

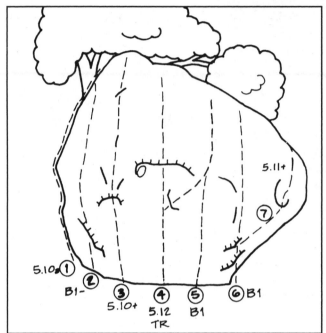

**B1 Boulder
West Face
Topo 7**

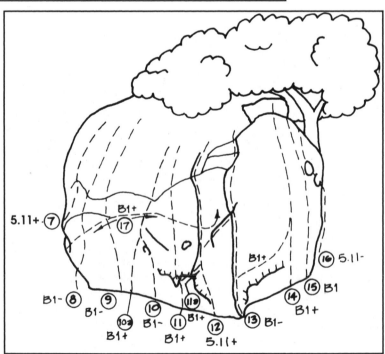

**B1 Boulder, South and East Faces
Topo 8**

B1 Boulder
(AKA Pink Floyd or Concert Rock),
West Face
Topo 7
1. **The Corner 5.10a** ★
2. **Corner II 5.11c**
3. **Hog Tied 5.10+** TR
4. **Slap your Puppet 5.12** TR
5. **Master of Reality B1** ★ Stem.
6. **Expansion Chamber B1** ★ OTD Direct arête.
7. **The Ear 5.11+**

B1 Boulder, South and East Faces
Topo 8
7. **The Ear 5.11+** Direct start is B1-
8. **Inside Out B1-** ★
9. **ELP B1-** ★
10. **Pink Floyd B1-** ★ Without cheatstone, B1.
10a. **Waugh Variation B1+** Start with left hand in low holds. Rated B2+ if started with right hand on low hold and cross over with left.
11. **Apesma B1+ Ed's variation B1+/B2** Sit down start.
11a. **Titty Fuck B1+/B2-** Low undercling. Start on tit, traverse to crack and up.
12. **The Crack 5.11+/B1-** ★
13. **Flying Circus B1-** ★
14. **Elimination Problem B1+**
15. **Neal Kaptain's Horror B1**
16. **Two Scoops 5.11-**
17. **Ed's Traverse B1+** Stay as low as possible.

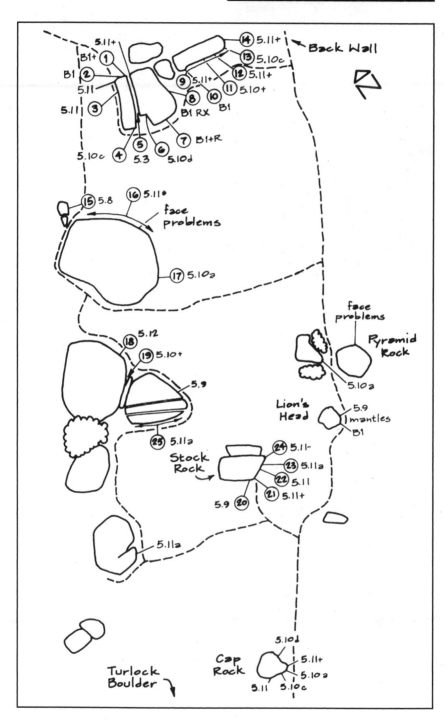

East Side Boulders, Map 9

East Side Boulders

Map 9

1. **Johnson Arête B1+**
2. **Vain Problem B1**
3. **Valdez 5.11**
4. **Arête Skeleton 5.10c** TR
5. **Split Rock Chimney 5.3**
6. **Split Decision 5.10d ★** TR
7. **Johnson Problem B1+ ★** R
8. **Supernatural B1** R/X
9. **Eat Out More Often 5.11+** Traverse. Eliminator Traverse B2 from right to left.
10. **Power Glide. AKA: Snot Here. B1 ★**
11. **Standard Route 5.10+**
12. **Tree Route 5.11+**
13. **Renaissance Problem 5.10c ★**
14. **Dynamic Duo 5.11+**
15. **Chouinard Friction Problem 5.8**
16. **Spiral Traverse 5.11 ★**
17. **Bold-During 5.10a**
18. **Sudden Impact 5.12 ★** TR Pin scars
19. **Pie Slice 5.10+ ★** Fist crack or lieback.
20. **Easy Money 5.9**
21. **Black Monday 5.11+**
22. **Black Friday 5.11**
23. **Bull Market 5.11a ★**
24. **Corner the Market 5.11- ★** 5.10a with cheat boulder start.
25. **Sugar Pops 5.11a**

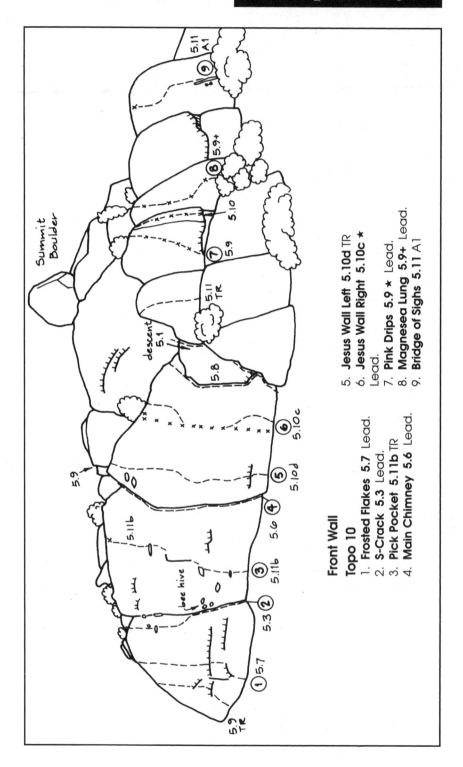

Front Wall

Topo 10

1. **Frosted Flakes 5.7** Lead.
2. **S-Crack 5.3** Lead.
3. **Pick Pocket 5.11b** TR
4. **Main Chimney 5.6** Lead.
5. **Jesus Wall Left 5.10d** TR
6. **Jesus Wall Right 5.10c** ★ Lead.
7. **Pink Drips 5.9** ★ Lead.
8. **Magnesea Lung 5.9+** Lead.
9. **Bridge of Sighs 5.11 A1**

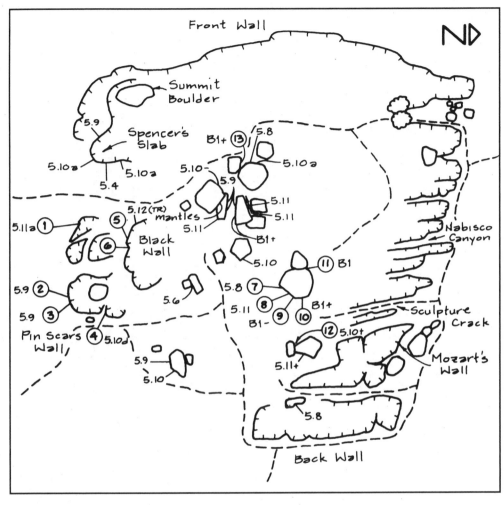

Summit Area
Map 11
1. **Packer Cracker 5.11a** TR
2. **Magnum Case 5.9**
3. **Machine Gun 5.9** ★ Two variations, can be led.
4. **Changeling 5.10d**
5. **Nose Cone 5.10+** ★
6. **Black Crack 5.9**
7. **Uma Gumma Crack 5.8**
8. **Hein Flake 5.11**
9. **Guarglophone B1-** ★
10. **Uma Gumma B1+** ★
11. **Roof Crack B1**
12. **Sticky Fingers 5.10+** Roof crack.
13. **Cry Uncle B1+**

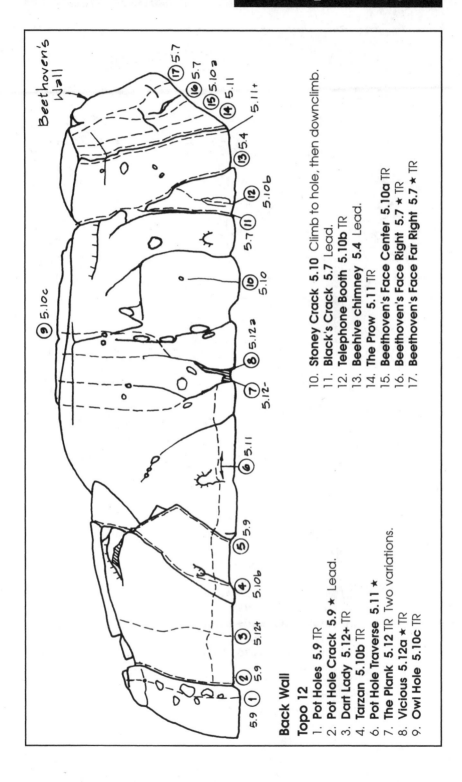

Beethoven's Wall

Back Wall

Topo 12

1. **Pot Holes** **5.9** TR
2. **Pot Hole Crack** **5.9** ★ Lead.
3. **Dart Lady** **5.12+** TR
4. **Tarzan** **5.10b** TR
6. **Pot Hole Traverse** **5.11** ★
7. **The Plank** **5.12** TR Two variations.
8. **Vicious** **5.12a** ★ TR
9. **Owl Hole** **5.10c** TR
10. **Stoney Crack** **5.10** Climb to hole, then downclimb.
11. **Black's Crack** **5.7** Lead.
12. **Telephone Booth** **5.10b** TR
13. **Beehive chimney** **5.4** Lead.
14. **The Prow** **5.11** TR
15. **Beethoven's Face Center** **5.10a** TR
16. **Beethoven's Face Right** **5.7** ★ TR
17. **Beethoven's Face Far Right** **5.7** ★ TR

Dimitri Fritz on "Mickey Mouse" (B1), Stoney Point.

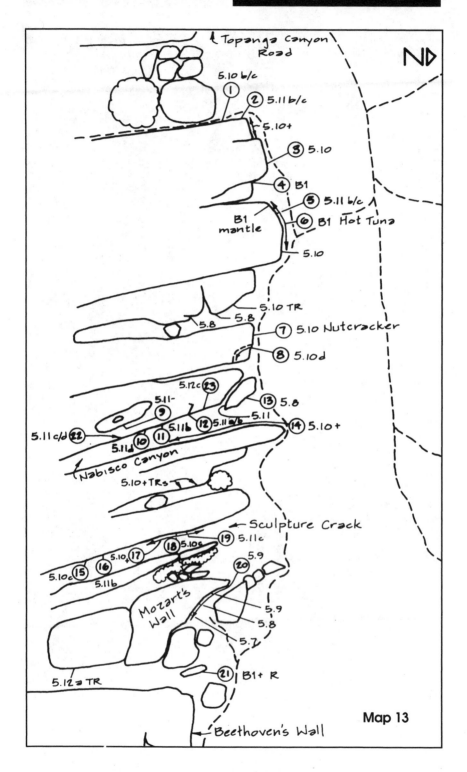

Topanga Canyon Road

N↓

Map 13

Beethoven's Wall

North Side Canyons
Map 13

1. **The Shark's Tooth 5.10 b/c** TR
2. **Land Shark 5.11 b/c** TR
3. **Undercling 5.10**
4. **Mickey Mouse B1**
5. **Cold Turkey 5.11 b/c**
6. **Hot Tuna B1** ★ Traverse
7. **Nutcracker 5.10** TR
8. **Cosmic Corner 5.10d** TR Traverse left under roof, then up.
9. **Anchor Cranker 5.11-**
10. **Iguana 5.11d** ★ TR
11. **Scurf 5.11b/c** TR
11a.**Gecko 5.12b** TR Start at Scurf, climb thin wall just left of Maggie's Farm.
12. **Maggie's Farm 5.11 a/b** ★ TR Several variations to the right and left.
13. **Texas Flake 5.8**
14. **Maggie's Traverse 5.10+**
15. **Sculpted Crack 5.10c**
16. **Carlsburg 5.11b** TR
17. **Sculpture Traverse 5.10+**
18. **Sculpture Crack 5.10c** ★ TR
19. **Sand Blast 5.11c** TR
20. **Mozart Wall Traverse 5.9**
21. **Plunger B1+** R
22. **Inside Line 5.11c/d** TR
23. **Sprout Wings and Fly 5.12c** TR

North Side Boulders

Map 14

1. **Standard Route 5.7** Descent route.
2. **Blunt Arête 5.10c**
3. **Bush Doctor 5.11b**
4. **Half Gram B1-** Mantel.
5. **The Chouinard Hole Problem 5.10-**
6. **Arête Me Not B1** ★
7. **Buckets to Bag Dad 5.11b**
8. **Bonehole 5.10**
9. **Sleazy Tabloid 5.11+**
10. **Slanderland 5.11** ★
11. **Bad Press B1-**
12. **Trouble Told 5.10-**
13. **Daily Circuit 5.10+**
14. **The 5.9 Slab 5.10c**
15. **The 5.10 Slab 5.10d**
16. **Holy ★?!# 5.10d** ★
17. **Reggae Route 5.10**
18. **Route Rustlin' 5.10**
19. **Yard the Tool 5.9**
20. **Hand Crack 5.11**
21. **Seam Stealer B1+**
22. **Scrambled Eggs Traverse 5.11+**
23. **Shorty Shea 5.10** OTD/R
24. **Beckus Memorial 5.10** OTD/R
25. **Incubus B1**
26. **Guar Scar B1** Seam
27. **Kodas Corner 5.11b/c** ★ Ground start rated B1.
28. **Flake to Nowhere 5.11b**
29. **Kodiak Corner 5.11b**
30. **Ozone Factor 5.11**
31. **Mantel Lobotomy 5.10+**
32. **Critter Crack 5.10**
33. **Yabo Arête B1/B1+** ★ R
34. **The Router Bit B1**
35. **Largonaut B1** Using block to start; B2 for ground start.
36. **Cleared for Takeoff B1+**
37. **The Roller Coaster 5.10+**
38. **Carousel Traverse B1** Traverses entire boulder.

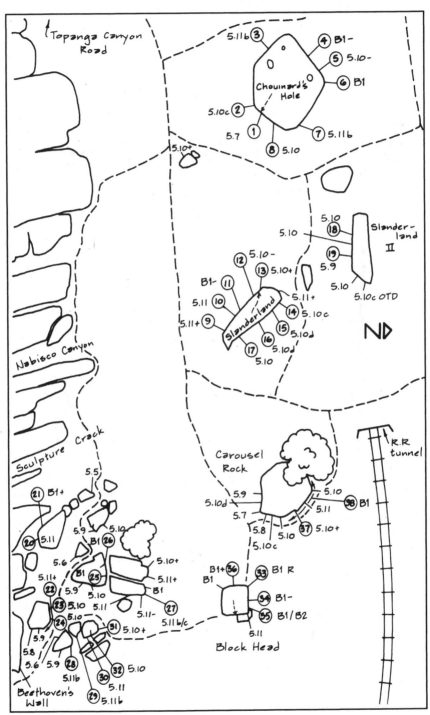

Map 14

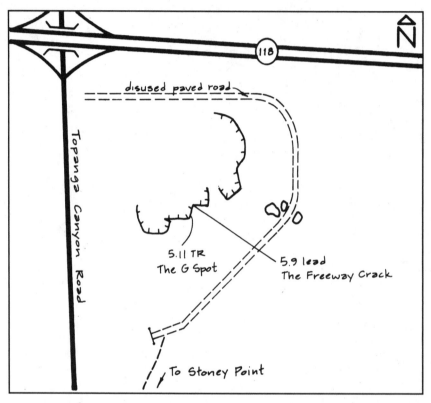

Freeway Crack Area, north of Stoney Point
Map 15

Outlying Areas Near Stoney Point.

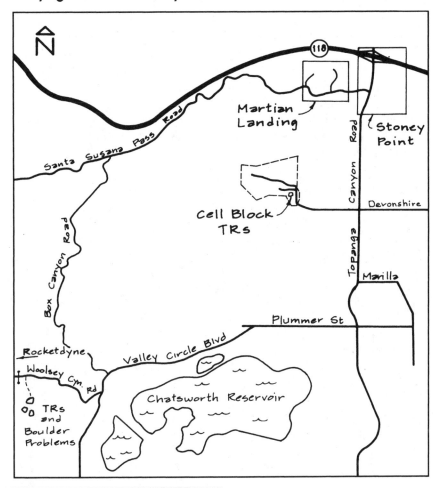

CHATSWORTH PARK SOUTH

The **Cell Block** in Chatsworth Park has two established top-ropes. The left (south) face is the **Escape Artist** (5.11a/b) and the east face (toward the road) has **Birdman from Alcatraz** (5.11+). More potential bouldering can be found farther up the trail west of the park.

WOOLSEY CANYON

Drive up Woolsey Canyon past Rocketdyne signs to the Rocketdyne gate and park. Just left of the road is the **Indian Boulder**, with many bouldering problems and top-ropes. Across the canyon is a roof crack above a right-facing corner which can be led; **Rocketdyne Roof** (5.11a, pro to 4").

MARTIAN LANDING

The Martian Landing, directly across Topanga Canyon Road, has a great
deal of accessible rock. A quick walk from the parking area brings
you to a boulder-covered ridge with many top-rope and boulder
routes The rock is not as solid as Stoney's, but this area does offer a
good diversion.

Directions: Park on Red Mesa Road and follow the dirt trail up to the
boulders on the hill to the west. The adventurous may also want to
check out the many potential routes on the cliff faces and boulders
east of the road.

Martian Landing Area

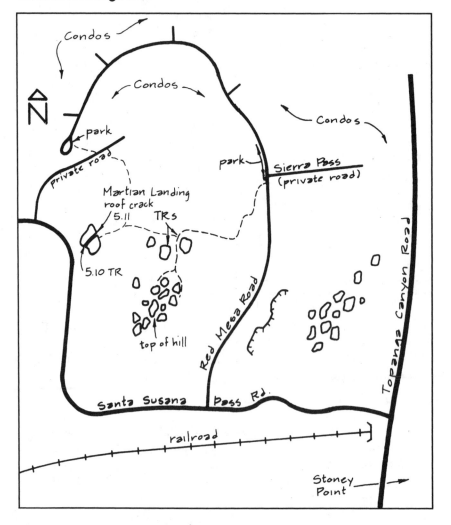

HORSE FLATS

Horse Flats is considered one of the best granite bouldering areas in
Southern California. Ideally placed in a mountain setting, large boulders cover the hillside above this tranquil campground. A short hike
up the trail leads to the main area where hundreds of classic problems have been done. The specialty of the area is arête climbing.
Varsity arête technique can easily be mastered after a couple of visits.
Another very attractive feature is the landings. The boulders are
spread out with flat , often soft landings which give that extra inspi-
ration for some of the OTD problems.

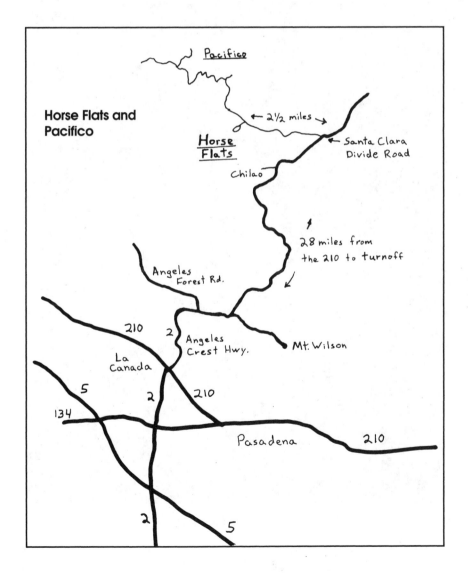

Todd Battey on the "Bow Sprits" (5.11), Horse Flats.

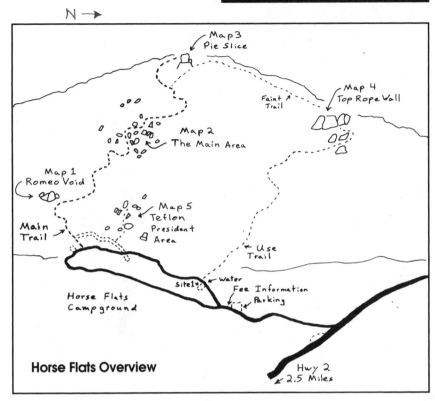

N →

Horse Flats Overview

Horse Flats was first explored as a climbing area in the early eighties. Mike Paul, Mike Guardino, Matt Dancy and Mike Ayon were the first to develop the bouldering. Soon after, many of L.A.'s local hotshots were heading there a couple of times a week, resulting in an abundance of hard, quality problems. The area has fallen out of popularity lately because Mt. Williamson is only a few more miles up the road which is an excellent sport climbing area.

Climbing is possible spring through fall. The area is at an elevation of about 5,000 feet and is an excellent escape from the heat and smog below. The road is closed in the winter due to snow.

PACIFICO

Bouldering is scattered around the Pacifico area and at the campground.

Directions: Follow the map to Horse Flats Campground. Go 1½ miles past the campground turnoff and take a left at a sign indicating Pacifico. Proceed for another 4.2 miles and make a right onto a dirt road. In another ½ mile a Pacific Crest Trail sign marks a road to the left which leads to the climbing area. This last section of the road may require 4-wheel drive.

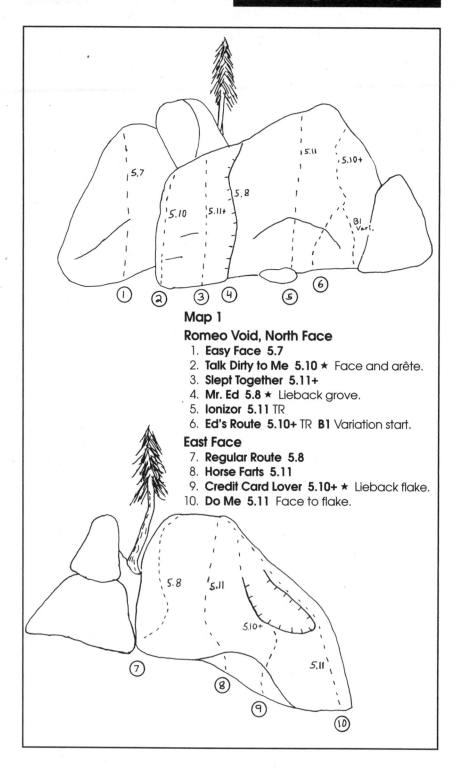

Map 1

Romeo Void, North Face
1. **Easy Face 5.7**
2. **Talk Dirty to Me 5.10** ★ Face and arête.
3. **Slept Together 5.11+**
4. **Mr. Ed 5.8** ★ Lieback grove.
5. **Ionizor 5.11** TR
6. **Ed's Route 5.10+** TR **B1** Variation start.

East Face
7. **Regular Route 5.8**
8. **Horse Farts 5.11**
9. **Credit Card Lover 5.10+** ★ Lieback flake.
10. **Do Me 5.11** Face to flake.

Craig Fry on the "Yard Arm" (5.11+), Horse Flats.
Photo by Maureen Battey.

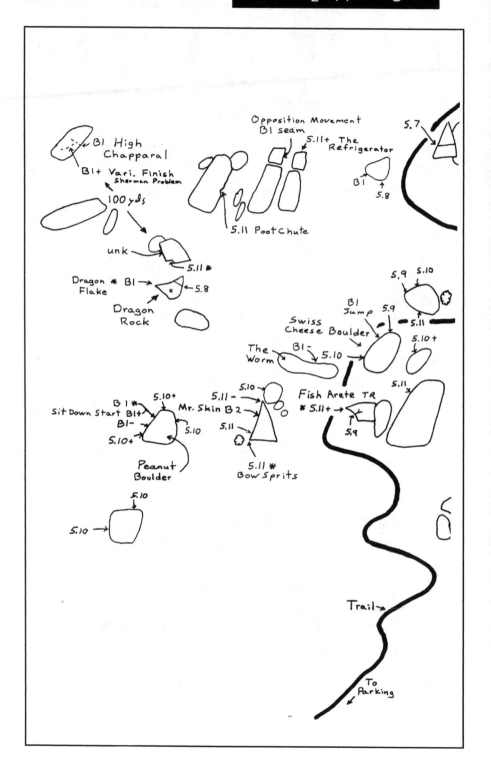

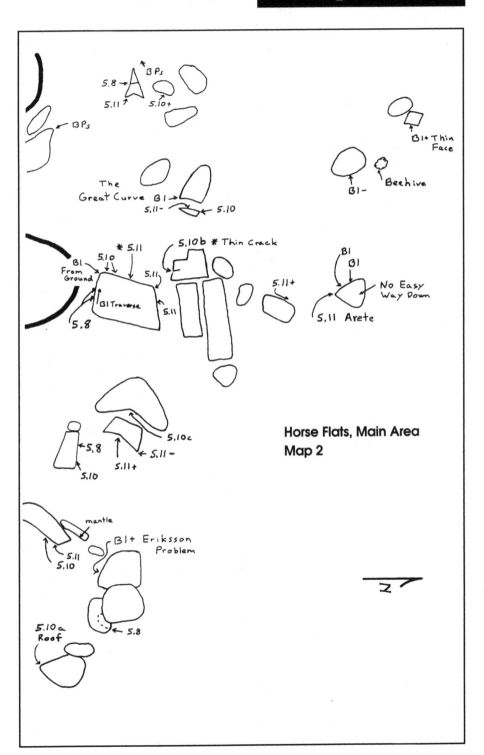

BPs

5.8 → BPs
5.11 ↗ 5.10+

BPs ←

B1+ Thin Face

The
Great Curve B1 →
5.11- ← 5.10

B1- Beehive

* 5.11
5.10b * Thin Crack
B1
From
Ground 5.10
5.11
5.11+ B1
B1
No Easy
Way Down
B1 Traverse 5.11
5.8 5.11 Arete

5.8 ←
5.10 5.11+
5.10c
← 5.11-

**Horse Flats, Main Area
Map 2**

mantle
B1+ Eriksson
Problem
5.11
5.10

N

5.10 a
Roof ← 5.8

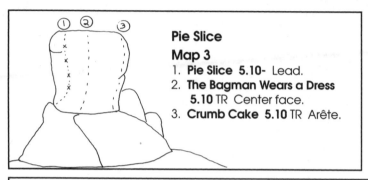

Pie Slice

Map 3
1. **Pie Slice 5.10-** Lead.
2. **The Bagman Wears a Dress 5.10** TR Center face.
3. **Crumb Cake 5.10** TR Arête.

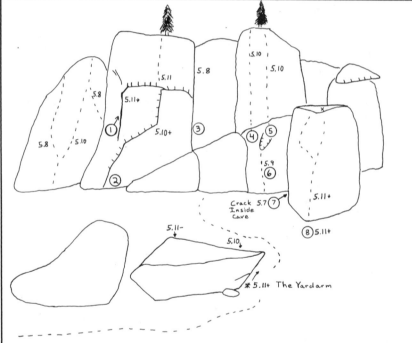

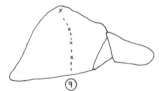

Top-Rope Wall, Map 4
1. **Horse Power 5.11+** TR Crack to traverse along roof to finish of Ant Line.
2. **Ant Line 5.11** ★ Lead or top rope. Lieback and undercling to face finish.

3. **Horse Play 5.8** Hands.
4. **Blackie's 5.10** TR
5. **Black and Blue 5.10** TR
6. **Flicka 5.9**
7. **Reed's Direct 5.7** ★ Crack inside cave; the chimney is off limits.
8. **Bat Flake Arête 5.11+** ★ TR
9. **Gray Matter 5.12a** Lead.

Fifty feet to the left of the Top Rope Wall are two top-rope routes: Harlem Shuffle 5.11. is a short crack to a roof. The other route starts off a chockstone and climbs a face 5.10. There is also more bouldering on the summit of the Top Rope Wall.

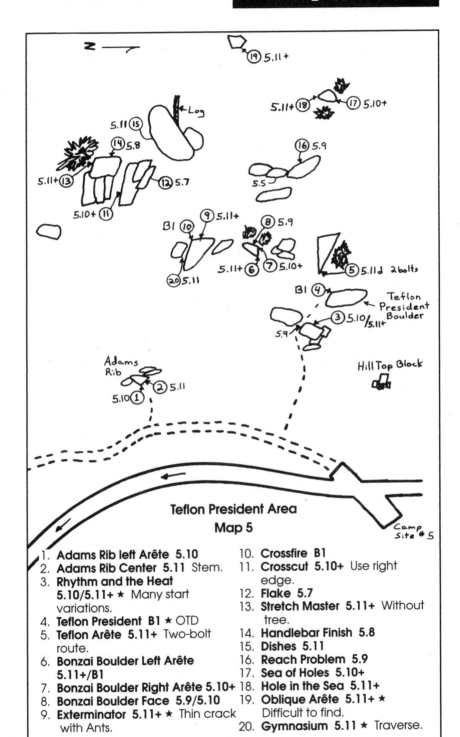

Teflon President Area

Map 5

1. **Adams Rib left Arête 5.10**
2. **Adams Rib Center 5.11** Stem.
3. **Rhythm and the Heat 5.10/5.11+** ★ Many start variations.
4. **Teflon President B1** ★ OTD
5. **Teflon Arête 5.11+** Two-bolt route.
6. **Bonzai Boulder Left Arête 5.11+/B1**
7. **Bonzai Boulder Right Arête 5.10+**
8. **Bonzai Boulder Face 5.9/5.10**
9. **Exterminator 5.11+** ★ Thin crack with Ants.
10. **Crossfire B1**
11. **Crosscut 5.10+** Use right edge.
12. **Flake 5.7**
13. **Stretch Master 5.11+** Without tree.
14. **Handlebar Finish 5.8**
15. **Dishes 5.11**
16. **Reach Problem 5.9**
17. **Sea of Holes 5.10+**
18. **Hole in the Sea 5.11+**
19. **Oblique Arête 5.11+** ★ Difficult to find.
20. **Gymnasium 5.11** ★ Traverse.

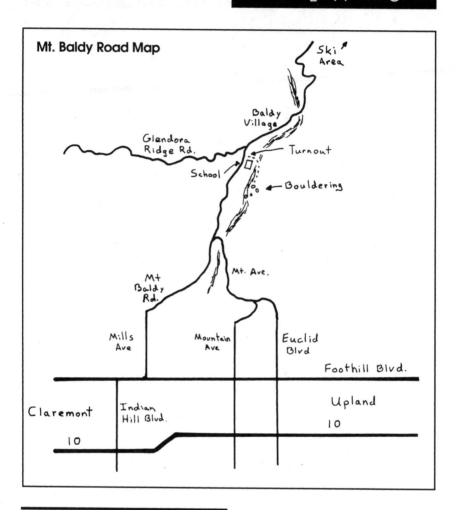

Mt. Baldy Road Map

Mt. Baldy

The **Mt. Baldy** bouldering area was a popular bouldering area but accessibility has been restricted at times because the area is on private property. The area was first developed by Paul Gleason, and then the Stonemasters, including John Long, Rick Accomazzo, Richard Harrison, Robs Muir and James Dutzi. The boulders are composed of river-polished granite composite with poor landings. Access problems have caused the area's popularity to fade, with many private property and keep out signs appearing before one reaches the lower boulders. The upper boulders are still on quasi-accessible property, but this area is very limited.

Directions: Park at the school and walk up the road to a turnout just past the school. Follow the trail down to the stream, and then downstream 100 yards until large boulders appear.

Orange County has several natural bouldering areas: **Corona del Mar, Turtle Rock** and the **Ortega Highway** areas. Another popular area is **Hart Park**, which has extensive artificial buildering walls that are climbable with no apparent access problems at this time.

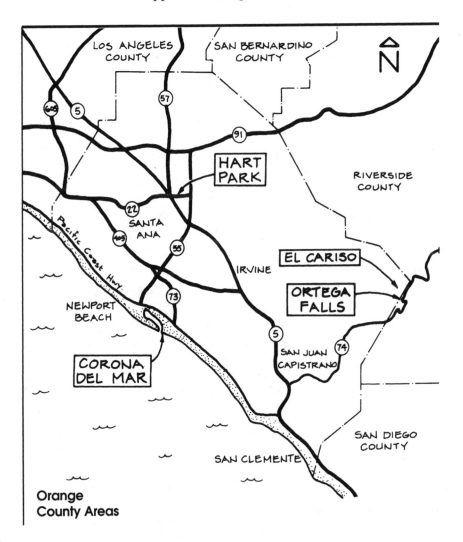

Orange
County Areas

HART PARK

The **Hart Park** walls have been a popular training area since the early seventies for climbers in Orange County. The original traverse on the upper retaining wall was probably one of the first bouldering walls to become popular and is characteristically very thin. This wall is located at the west end of the park and the climbing is on the textured blocks used to build the wall. Dan Leichtfuss was the first to complete the entire traverse. More climbing walls can be found down Santiago Creek under Glassel and the 22.

Warning: The thin edges and long traverses have contributed to many cases of finger tendonitis.

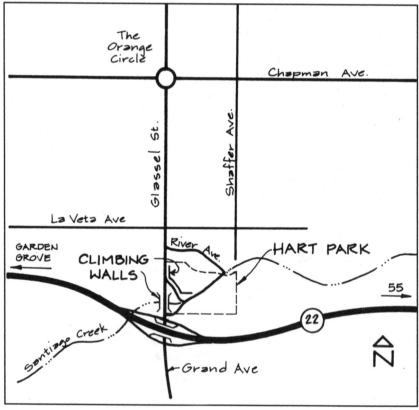

Hart Park Road Map

CORONA DEL MAR

Corona del Mar, also known as **"The Beach"** or **"Pirate's Cove"** is the finest natural bouldering area in Orange County. The Beach is a small cove with a 12- to 35-foot high cliff band just inside the jetty of Newport Bay. It's important to realize that the rock quality is very dependent on local weather conditions, which can make the climbing miserable on a bad day. The rock is a knobby sandstone that tends to absorb a lot of water and grease. Therefore, it is suggested to climb only on days when the rock has received a lot of recent sunshine. Optimum conditions will be found on warm, fogless days from spring until fall. Also, high tides can flood the cave area, so use of a tide table is recommended. In summer, the lifeguards enforce a no climbing rule until after 5:00 p.m. for the safety of the beachgoers.

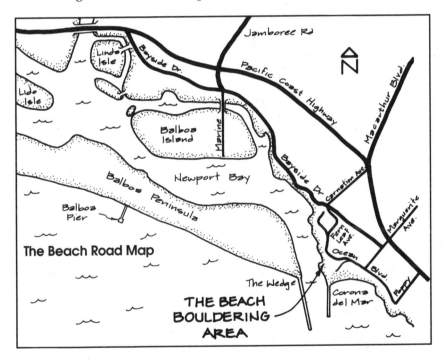

The Beach Road Map

The Beach was first discovered for climbing in the early seventies by Mike Graham (Gramicci), who, with the help of Rick Accomazzo, Robs Muir and Steve West, went on to clean and work out most of the classic problems. Spencer Lennard, Randy Vogel, Craig Fry and Dave Evans were also active in establishing problems up until the early eighties. The mid-eighties saw little new development other than the re-establishing of problems on which holds had broken off. In the late eighties, Rob Mulligan brought new vigor to the scene and broke the B2 barrier with his Sandman combination and Arabesque.

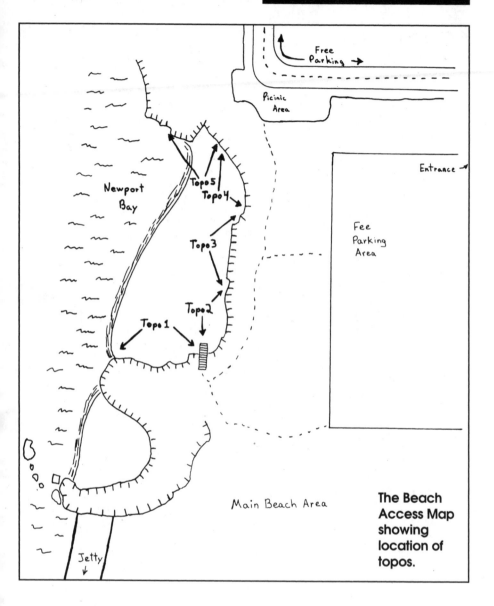

The Beach
Access Map
showing
location of
topos.

The climbing at The Beach is characterized by steep to overhanging jugs above the sand. A crowd of locals usually gathers after work in the summer, and many have the place ruthlessly wired. Tourists also gather to watch the crazy climbers and often feel compelled to applaud after any boulderer succeeds in topping out on a problem.

Recommended equipment for climbing at the beach: toothbrush, large extendo brush, extra chalk, a piece of carpet and a towel to wipe the sand out of your eyes.

Spencer Lennard on the "Italian Fall" (5.11+) at Corona Del Mar in 1977.

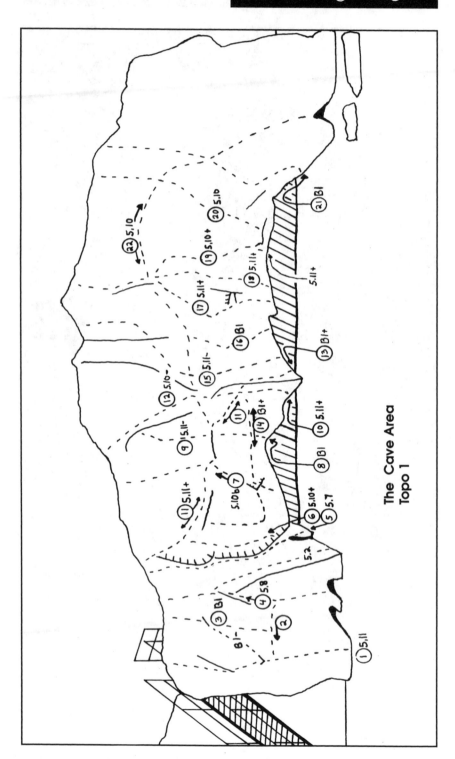

The Cave Area
Topo 1

The Cave Area, Topo 1

1. **Little Ricky 5.11** ★ Direct start B1 when sand is low.
2. **Traverse Start to Little Ricky 5.11+**
3. **Big Ricky B1**
4. **Baby Ricky 5.8**
5. **Lieback 5.7**
6. **Gather Up 5.10+** Slab is off-limits.
7. **Onion Man 5.10b** ★
8. **Diamond Man B1** ★ Cave start.
9. **Diamond Man Dyno 5.11-** Direct Finish
10. **Iron Man Roof 5.11+** ★ Cave start.
11. **Iron Man Traverse 5.11+**
11a. **Full Iron Man B1+** ★ Combine cave start with traverse.
12. **Tin Man 5.10-** Start above cave.
13. **Nowhere Man B1+** Cave start.
14. **Sand Man Traverse B1+**
14a. **Full Sand Man B2** Combine Nowhere Man start and Sand Man Traverse.
15. **Sand Gully 5.11-** Dirty.
16. **Hard but Lennard B1**
17. **The Clit 5.11+/B1**
18. **The Parlor 5.11+**
19. **High Over Beached Whales 5.10+** Cave start is **5.11+**.
20. **The Shelf 5.10**
21. **Hot Stuff B1** Cave start.
22. **High Noon Traverse 5.10**

Craig Fry on the "Iron Man Roof" (5.11+) at Corona Del Mar.
Photo by Dean Kubani.

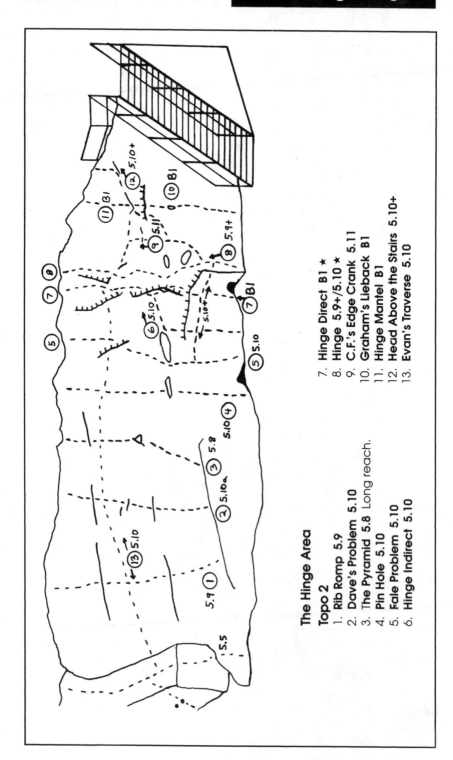

The Hinge Area

Topo 2

1. Rib Romp 5.9
2. Dave's Problem 5.10
3. The Pyramid 5.8 Long reach.
4. Pin Hole 5.10
5. Fale Problem 5.10
6. Hinge Indirect 5.10
7. Hinge Direct B1 ★
8. Hinge 5.9+/5.10 ★
9. C.F.'s Edge Crank 5.11
10. Graham's Lieback B1
11. Hinge Mantel B1
12. Head Above the Stairs 5.10+
13. Evan's Traverse 5.10

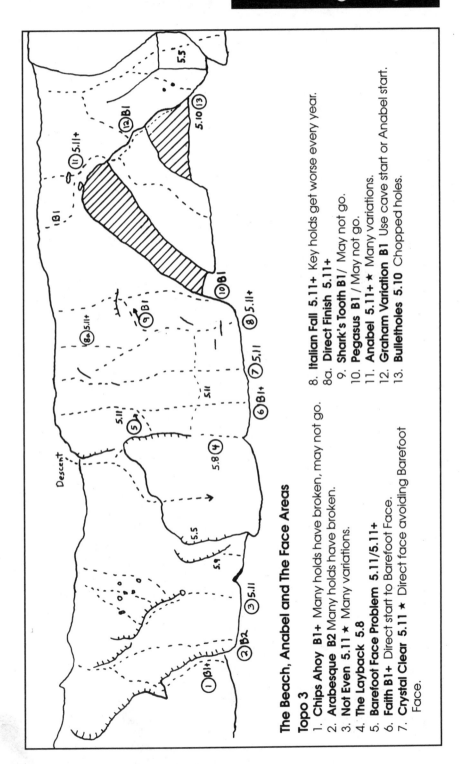

The Beach, Anabel and The Face Areas

Topo 3

1. **Chips Ahoy B1+** Many holds have broken, may not go.
2. **Arabesque B2** Many holds have broken.
3. **Not Even 5.11 ★** Many variations.
4. **The Layback 5.8**
5. **Barefoot Face Problem 5.11/5.11+**
6. **Faith B1+** Direct start to Barefoot Face.
7. **Crystal Clear 5.11 ★** Direct face avoiding Barefoot Face.
8. **Italian Fall 5.11+** Key holds get worse every year.
8a. **Direct Finish 5.11+**
9. **Shark's Tooth B1/** May not go.
10. **Pegasus B1/** May not go.
11. **Anabel 5.11+ ★** Many variations.
12. **Graham Variation B1** Use cave start or Anabel start.
13. **Bulletholes 5.10** Chopped holes.

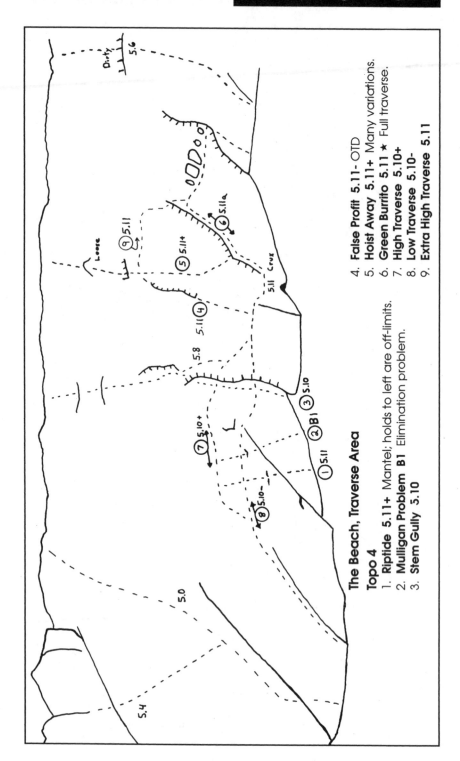

The Beach, Traverse Area

Topo 4

1. **Riptide 5.11+** Mantel; holds to left are off-limits.
2. **Mulligan Problem B1** Elimination problem.
3. **Stem Gully 5.10**
4. **False Profit 5.11-** OTD
5. **Hoist Away 5.11+** Many variations.
6. **Green Burrito 5.11** ★ Full traverse.
7. **High Traverse 5.10+**
8. **Low Traverse 5.10-**
9. **Extra High Traverse 5.11**

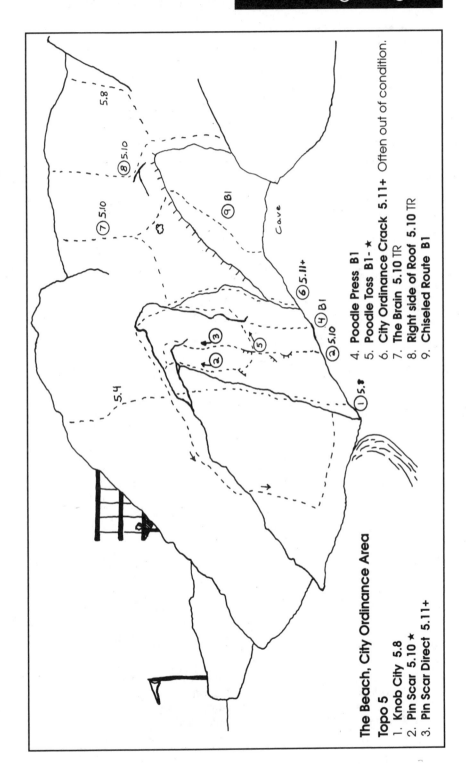

The Beach, City Ordinance Area

Topo 5
1. Knob City 5.8
2. Pin Scar 5.10 ★
3. Pin Scar Direct 5.11+

4. Poodle Press B1
5. Poodle Toss B1- ★
6. City Ordinance Crack 5.11+ Often out of condition.
7. The Brain 5.10 TR
8. Right side of Roof 5.10 TR
9. Chiseled Route B1

TURTLE ROCK

Turtle Rock is a small bouldering area in the city of Irvine. This small overhanging outcrop has a city park built around it with a manicured lawn tight up to the base. At first glance the rock appears to be quite poor but closer inspection reveals it to be made up of a solid matrix of bits and pieces of shells and sand bonded together with limestone, which makes for good, but limited climbing.

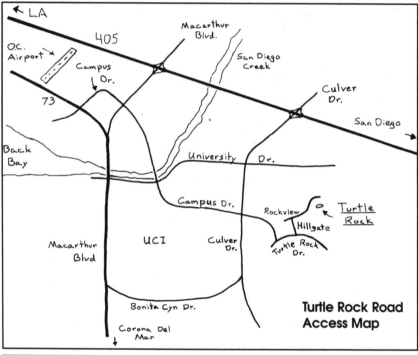

Turtle Rock Road Access Map

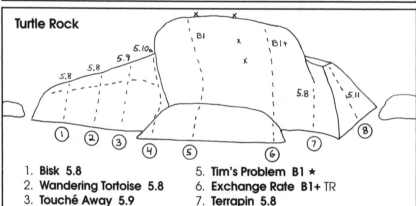

Turtle Rock

1. **Bisk 5.8**
2. **Wandering Tortoise 5.8**
3. **Touché Away 5.9**
4. **Cornered 5.10** ★
5. **Tim's Problem B1** ★
6. **Exchange Rate B1+** TR
7. **Terrapin 5.8**
8. **Turtle Soup 5.11**

EL CARISO

The **El Cariso** bouldering area is a chaparral-engulfed hillside covered with beautiful polished granite boulders. The rock and climbing characteristics are very similar to **Santee**. But unlike Santee, the boulders are immersed in a thick sea of chaparral and access can be quite difficult. Small holds, rounded mantels, seams, arêtes and friction are the standard fare for these boulders. Check out the **Cling or Fling** area for the highest quality rock. The area was first discovered after a fire swept the hills clean and the white boulders stood out like a beacon to local climbers. Brady Willitson and Dean Goolsby were the first explorers to ferret out the bouldering and top-roping potential. The area was popular for a couple of years, but soon faded as the thick brush grew back.

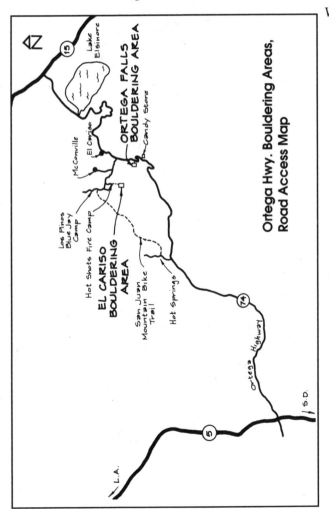

With the area now being described in a guidebook, it's bound to become popular again. Hopefully, some locals will take it upon themselves to clear trails into the area and around the boulders. The most important trail that needs to be cleared is a trail circumnavigating the fire station as shown on the map as "proposed trail." This trail would help alleviate any access problems with the Hot Shot Camp personnel who are quite paranoid of people going into the area and possibly starting fires. The proposed trail would start at the main road and connect to the fire break on top of the ridge. Check to see if the trail is there first. If it is not, then please walk through the Hot Shot Camp as unobtrusively as possible.

The El Cariso area is quite warm in the summer months, but late afternoons would be a good time to visit. Fall and winter are the recommended time of year because the chaparral growth would be receding. Be on the look out for concealed poison oak and snakes.

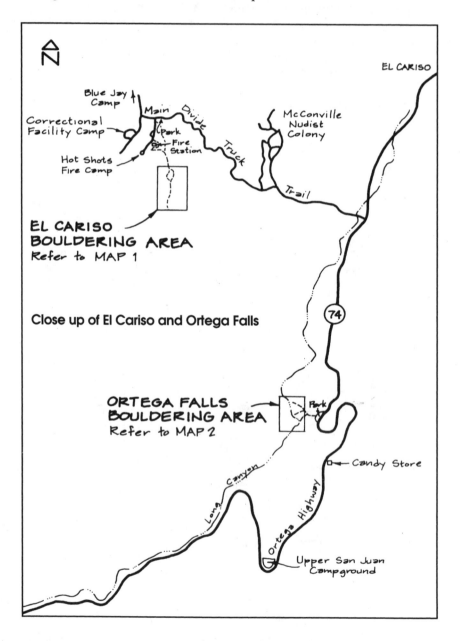

Close up of El Cariso and Ortega Falls

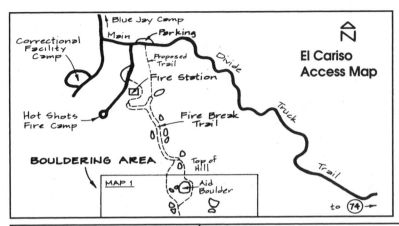

El Cariso
Access Map

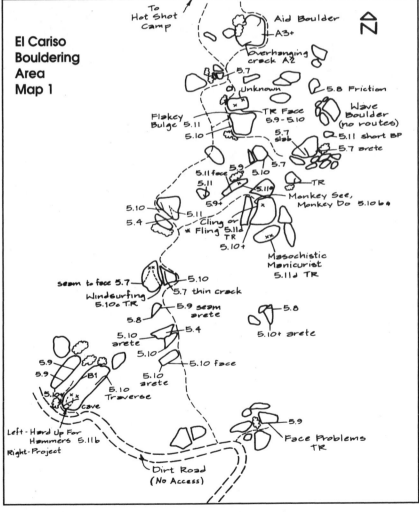

El Cariso
Bouldering
Area
Map 1

ORTEGA FALLS

Ortega Falls is a beautiful natural area with flowing waterfalls and water-polished granite bouldering and climbing. The area is just off the road and, unfortunately, attracts a lot a tourists. The climbing is good, but limited, and is quite popular with intermediate climbers. The polished rock is so slick that even the most advanced climbers will keep checking their boots to figure out why they can't stand on any small footholds.

The area has seen rock climbing activity since the early sixties. Many of the routes were aid climbs then, and old bolts and pin scars are common. The main detraction to the area for climbers is it's popularity with partiers, bikers, and tourists. During weekends, there may be 30 to 50 people in the small area and it's best to avoid it during this time. The best time to visit is on weekdays and evenings during the temperate months. The area can be very hot during the summer. Also avoid the area after rainy periods or the stream will be too high for climbing. Poison oak grows everywhere along the streambed.

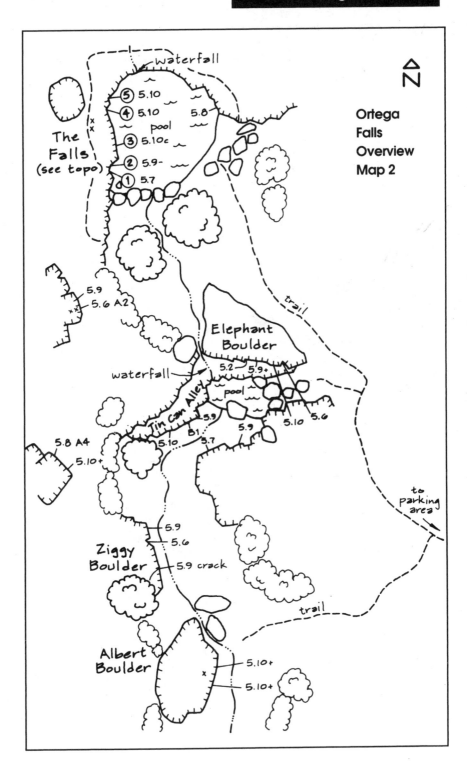

waterfall

⑤ 5.10
④ 5.10   5.8

The
Falls   pool
(see topo)   ③ 5.10c
              ② 5.9-
              ① 5.7

N

Ortega
Falls
Overview
Map 2

5.9
5.6 A2

Elephant
Boulder

trail

waterfall   5.2   5.9+

                   pool

Tin Can Alley   5.9   5.10 5.6
5.8 A4   5.10 .81 5.7   5.9
5.10+

to
parking
area

5.9
5.6

Ziggy
Boulder   5.9 crack

Albert
Boulder   5.10+

               5.10+

trail

ORTEGA FALLS WALL

The **Ortega Falls Wall** is usually top-roped but the routes can also be led. The wall is approximately 40-feet high to the first ledge and the anchors are about 12 feet higher. Two bolts without hangers are on top. It's recommended that you bring friends (size 2 and 2½), some stoppers and about ten feet of slings to back up the bolts (loop wireds over the studs). When the water is flowing, a pendulum is required to reach some of the routes.

**Topo of the
Ortega Falls Wall**
1. **5.7** Gully.
2. **5.9** ★ Thin crack.
3. **5.10c** First move is crux.
4. **5.10** Steep gully to overhang.
5. **5.10** Start to the right of Route 4 and climb the right side of the upper block.

falls →

5.7 ① ②   ③   ④   ⑤ 5.10
        5.9- 5.10c   5.10

pool

Inyo County is a very large area with a wealth of quality rock, notably the Sierra Nevada. As far as bouldering is concerned, the exceptional **Buttermilk** in Bishop is one of the finest bouldering areas in California but is beyond the scope of this Southern California guide. A description of the area was contained in *The Sierra East Side* by Alan Bartlett and Errett Allen, now out of print. The four areas covered in this book are: **The Coso Boulders, Fossil Falls, Little Lake Bouldering Walls** and **The Black Planets.**

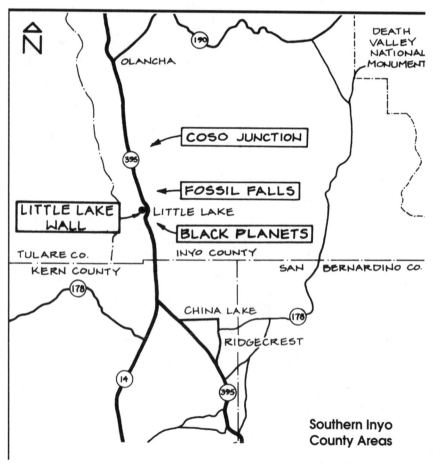

Southern Inyo County Areas

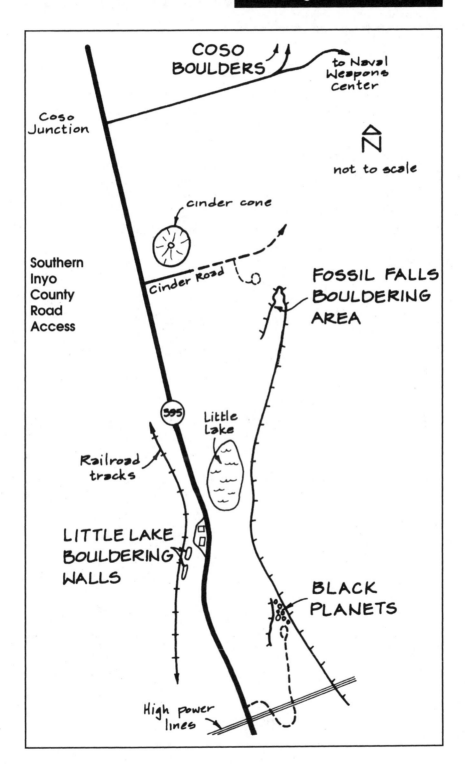

THE COSO BOULDERS

This remote bouldering area is a great place to go to hike, explore, and
boulder. The abundant rock is very similar to Joshua Tree quartz
monzonite and the boulder-covered hillsides stretch as far as the eye
can see. Unfortunately, the boulders are very rounded with few features, but many good boulder problems can be found. From the parking area at **Pictograph Rock,** walk north to the **Big Plate Rock.**
Several other problems and top-rope routes can be found in this area.

Probably the best attraction at this area is exploration. The abandoned
mining operation, Indian pictographs and thousands of boulders will
provide more than a day or two of fascination.

The Coso boulders are at about 5,000 feet elevation and best visited in
the moderate temperature months. The dirt road into the area is not
particularly bad, but would not be recommended for vehicles with
low clearance.

For additional information on this area see *Southern Sierra Rock Climbing:
Domelands* by Sally Moser and Greg Vernon, published by
Chockstone Press.

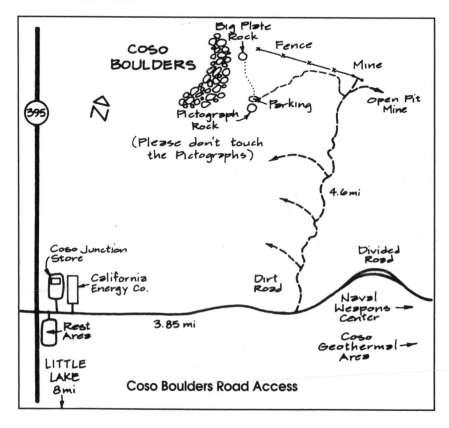

Coso Boulders Road Access

FOSSIL FALLS BOULDERING AREA

Fossil Falls is another great place to visit for bouldering or climbing
while driving highway 395. The area is better-known for top-rope
and short sport climbing routes. The rock is a polished columnar
basalt with numerous flakes, pockets, and seams. Many boulder
problems can be found along the base of the cliffs and around the
falls area on the ultra-polished rock. The bouldering wall shown on
the topo is at the lower end of the west wall. The cliff is approximately 12 to 25 feet at this section and offers quality bouldering for
advanced climbers. Many climbers may be inclined to use a top-rope
for some of the routes described.

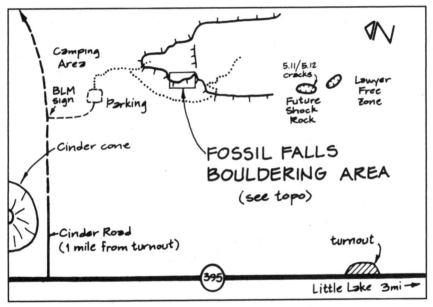

Fossil Falls Bouldering Area

The name Fossil Falls is actually a misnomer: the water source was cut
off in this century, with the building of the L.A. aqueduct. Before that
time, water flowed from Owens Lake and formed the steep-walled
canyon. Indian pictographs and artifacts can be found with a little
exploration around this area—Please don't disturb them!

The area is at about 3,500 feet elevation and can be quite hot in the summer months. Primitive camping is available anywhere around the
area except the main parking lot. For climbing route information see
Southern Sierra Rock Climbing: Domelands by Sally Moser and Greg
Vernon, published by Chockstone Press.

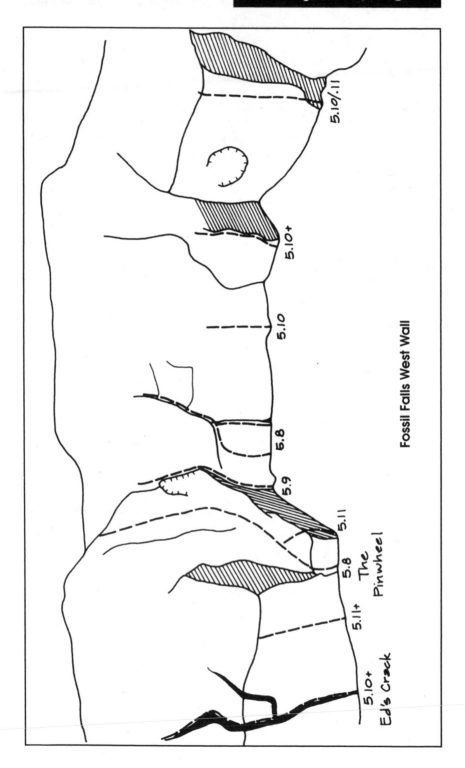

Fossil Falls West Wall

LITTLE LAKE BOULDERING WALLS

Just south of the town of Little Lake are two short volcanic bluffs by the side of the road. The walls sport several boulder problems and short (30-feet) routes. Most of the routes are crack climbs and can be soloed by advanced climbers. Top-ropes can also be set up easily for climbers willing to spend any amount of time here.

The walls face southeast and bake during the hotter months. A good time to visit is during that long drive on 395 when a quick workout is just what you need to get your blood flowing enough to make it a couple more hours on the road.

THE BLACK PLANETS

The Black Planets is a group of boulders that have tumbled down from the volcanic rim into the sandy wash below. The rock is basalt similar to Fossil Falls and Little Lake. The area shown on the map consists of about ten boulders from 8 to 15 feet high. The area is actually quite limited with only about 10 to 20 good bouldering routes. A short wall on the west side of the parking area has several additional top-rope and bouldering routes. More good bouldering can be found when exploring either direction at the base of the rim.

The elevation is 3,000 feet and the area is very hot during summer months. Visit during moderate temperatures.

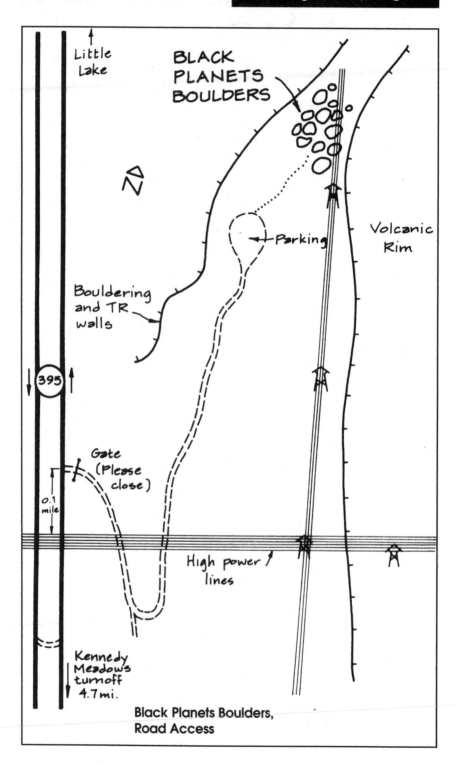

Little
Lake

BLACK
PLANETS
BOULDERS

N↗

Volcanic
Rim

Parking

Bouldering
and TR
walls

395

Gate
(Please
close)

0.1
mile

High power
lines

Kennedy
Meadows
turnoff
4.7 mi.

**Black Planets Boulders,
Road Access**

San Bernardino County, the largest county in California, is actually larg-
er than many states. Most of the county is desert, and there is
undoubtedly much rock waiting to be discovered and explored. At
present, however, few climbers have explored the vast expanses
beyond sight of the highways. Four San Bernardino county areas are
described in this book: **Wagon Wheel, Mentone, Giant Rock**, and
Joshua Tree. Joshua Tree is only partly in San Bernardino County.
Most of the bouldering is actually in Riverside County, but it is
placed in this part of the book for convenience. Giant Rock is nearby
and is a pleasant diversion from Joshua Tree for new problems or to
escape the cold. Wagon Wheel is located at the very northern edge of
San Bernardino County, near Ridgecrest. It is a fine area to visit on
the way to the Eastern Sierra.

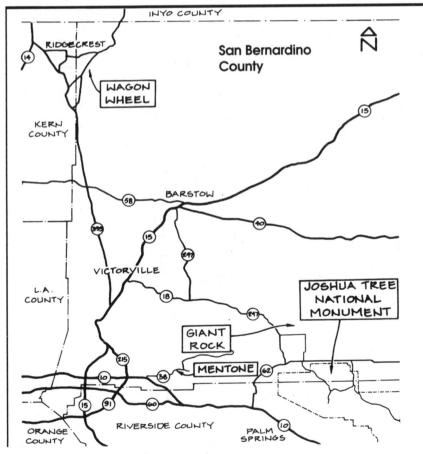

WAGON WHEEL

The **Wagon Wheel** bouldering area is perhaps one of the finest granite bouldering areas in Southern California. It is a city of boulders stretching as far as the eye can see and is far from being totally explored. This guide only covers the central area of the expanse and exploration north and east will reveal many new treasures. The rock is a compact quartz diorite that is highly textured with weathered patina, knobs, and flakes.

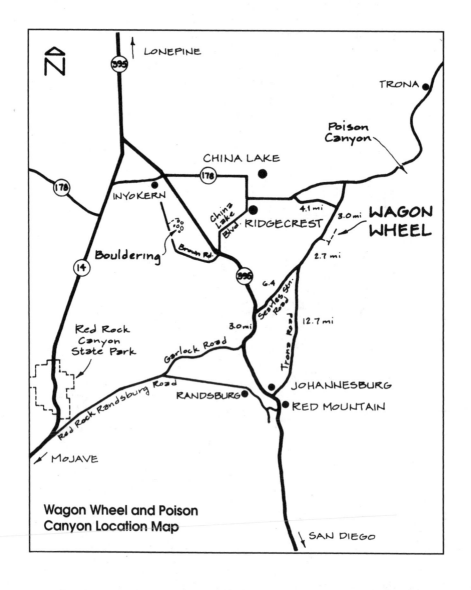

Wagon Wheel and Poison Canyon Location Map

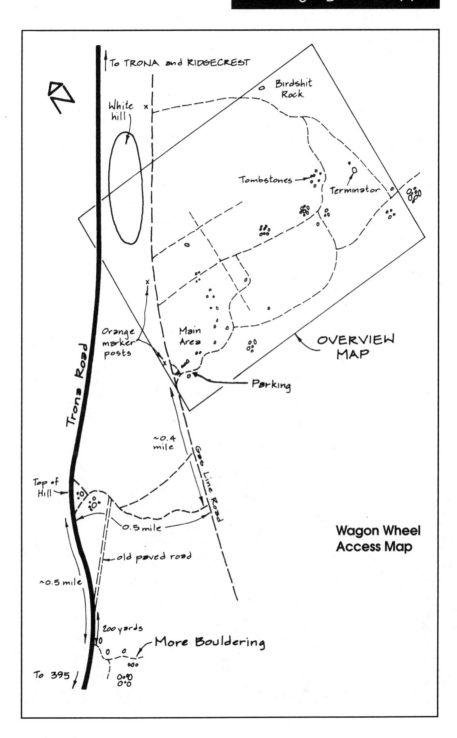

To TRONA and RIDGECREST

Birdshit Rock

White hill

Tombstones

Terminator

Trona Road

Orange marker posts

Main Area

OVERVIEW MAP

Parking

~0.4 mile

Gas Line Road

Top of Hill

0.5 mile

old paved road

~0.5 mile

200 yards

More Bouldering

To 395

Wagon Wheel Access Map

The main area adjacent to the parking area shown has a plethora of short quality problems. A short hike (or drive) to the **Tombstone** area puts you at the center of the B1 capitol of Wagon Wheel. Tall boulders with sensational hard problems can be found in abundance. Only the most significant problems are shown on the maps. Some of the boulder problems here have been turned into very short sport climbs with 2 or 3 bolts. Hopefully this trend will not continue. The maps also point out some boulderfields that have been named but not developed.

Wagon Wheel is a BLM off-road use area and offers excellent camping (no facilities). Mountain bikes are useful for exploration.

Season: Wagon Wheel lies at an elevation of 3,500 feet and the season is fall through spring. Late evenings in the summer are also good, but during the day the rock sizzles in the scorching desert sun. For more information see *Southern Sierra Rock Climbing: Domelands* by Sally Moser and Greg Vernon, published by Chockstone Press.

Todd Battey on "Still Life Arete" (5.10) at Wagon Wheel.

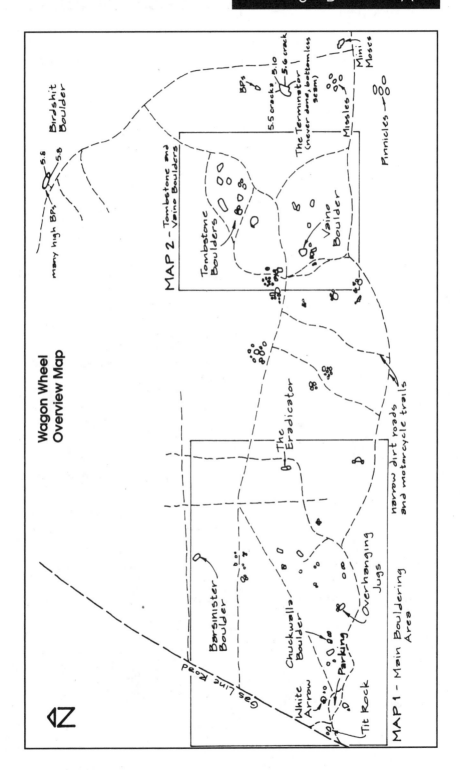

Wagon Wheel
Overview Map

Birdshit
Boulder

many high BP's

5.8
5.8

BP's

5.5 crack 5.10
5.6 crack

The Terminator
(never done, bottomless
seam)

Missiles

Mini
Moses

Pinnacles

MAP 2 - Tombstone and
Vaino Boulders

Tombstone
Boulders

Vaino
Boulder

The Eradicator

narrow dirt roads
and motorcycle trails

Barsinister
Boulder

Chuckwalla
Boulder

Overhanging
Jugs

Parking

White Arrow

Tit Rock

MAP 1 - Main Bouldering
Area

Gas Line Road

N

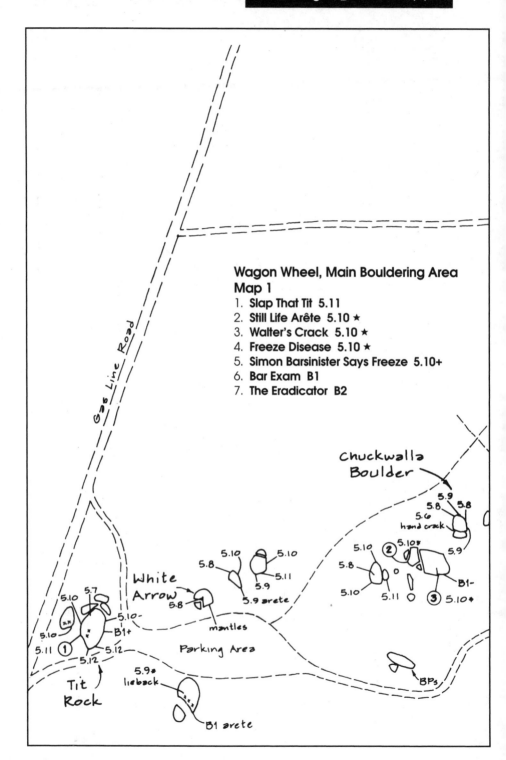

Wagon Wheel, Main Bouldering Area Map 1

1. **Slap That Tit 5.11**
2. **Still Life Arête 5.10 ★**
3. **Walter's Crack 5.10 ★**
4. **Freeze Disease 5.10 ★**
5. **Simon Barsinister Says Freeze 5.10+**
6. **Bar Exam B1**
7. **The Eradicator B2**

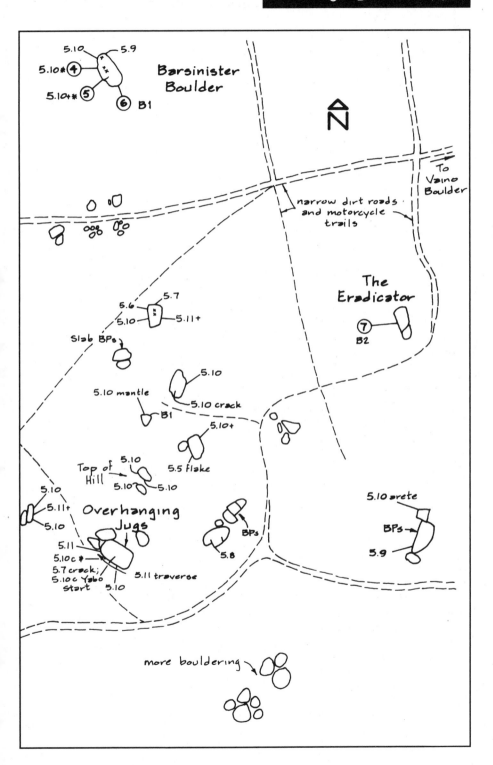

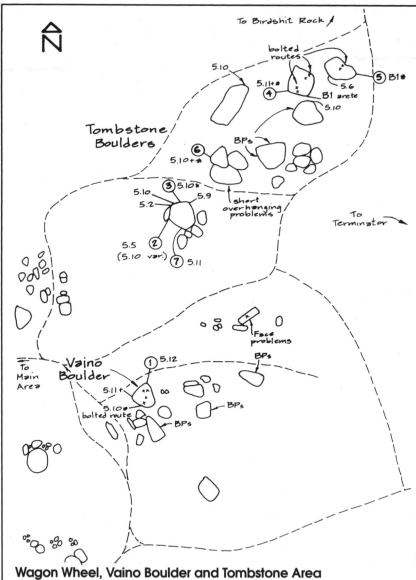

Wagon Wheel, Vaino Boulder and Tombstone Area
Map 2
1. **The Eliminator 5.12** TR
2. **Onion Skin 5.5** Dihedral. **Buttercup Variation 5.10** OTD lieback. undercling and finish.
3. **Solid Garnish 5.10★** Face.
4. **The Flake Collector 5.11+★**
5. **Tombstone Arête B1★**
6. **Rock Wrestling 5.10+★** Overhanging arête next to lower boulder.
7. **Butterfingers 5.11**

POISON CANYON

Northeast of Wagon Wheel, Highway 178 passes through **Poison Canyon** with 40- to 60-foot cliffs of quartz diorite along both sides of the road. An inland sea once covered this region and has left thick deposits of calcium carbonate in the cracks and on the rocks. This layer must sometimes be cleaned off to reveal quality climbing. The area offers short leads, top-roping and limited bouldering. **See map on page 112 for location.**

THE MENTONE BOULDERS

The Mentone Boulders is a small climbing area located at a picnic area just outside Mentone. The area consists of one boulder with several problems and a small crag with a bolted route and a couple of top-ropes. The rock is a curious metamorphic that has been water-polished. To reach the area, drive north on Highway 38 to the picnic area on the south side of the road just before Mountain Home Village. Park and walk across the streambed to the boulders on the far southwestern end. **See San Bernardino County Map on page 111 for location.**

GIANT ROCK

Giant Rock is an excellent bouldering area, well worth a visit when you're staying in Joshua Tree. The lower elevation could be a welcome relief on a cold winter day. The rock is granite covered with a thick varnish which has the feel of sculpted steel. Abundant flakes and edges provide excellent steep and overhanging face problems with sandy bases. The hills are covered with huge boulders with excellent bouldering potential.

The Giant Rock boulder has many Glue-on routes, but many (or all) may not go at this time because of broken holds. The creators used substandard glue and many holds broke off while they were first climbing them. Since then, many holds have been chopped, shot at, and painted over. The **DMZ** is a new sport climbing area with over 13 routes. The area is about ¼ mile past the Giant Rock just behind the Sand Hill. It is also referred to as **Sandy Cove**.

On a more curious note, Giant Rock is reported to be an area of frequent UFO sightings. According to legend, George Van Tassel is credited with having established communication with the alien travelers. He then set out to build the "Integratron," as specified in instructions he received from the space beings. The Integratron's purpose was to provide human and alien alike with special rejuvenating powers.

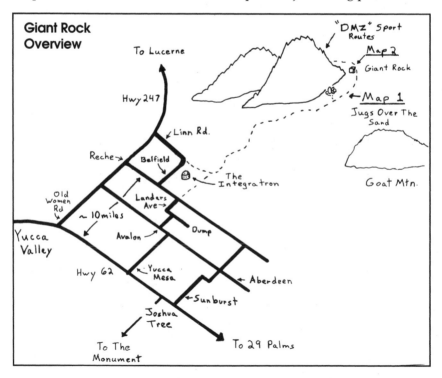

Giant Rock Overview

To Lucerne

"DMZ" Sport Routes

Map 2

Giant Rock

Hwy 247

Map 1
Jugs Over The Sand

Linn Rd.

Reche → Belfield

The Integratron

Goat Mtn.

Old Women Rd.

Landers Ave →

~10 miles

Avalon →

Dump

Yucca Valley

Hwy 62

Yucca Mesa

Aberdeen

← Sunburst

Joshua Tree

To The Monument

To 29 Palms

Adding more mystery to the legend, Van Tassel was killed by persons unknown shortly after he supposedly learned of the last remaining component to power the device.

The area is on BLM land and good primitive camping is available, but it sustains heavy abuse from motorcyclists, four-wheelers, and gun lovers, resulting in an overabundance of trash and noise. It might be best to avoid this area on holiday weekends when hostile types may be camped at the base of the rock. The area also attracts worshippers of a different bent, and rumor has it that on full moons many strange things go down out there.

Season: The elevation is about 3,000 feet and is therefore warmer than Joshua Tree. Climbing is best fall through spring.

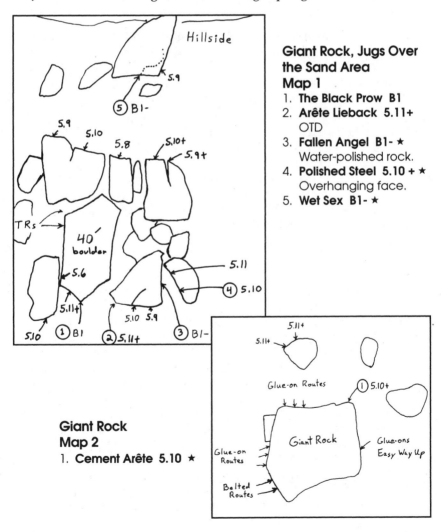

Giant Rock, Jugs Over the Sand Area
Map 1
1. **The Black Prow B1**
2. **Arête Lieback 5.11+** OTD
3. **Fallen Angel B1-** ★ Water-polished rock.
4. **Polished Steel 5.10 +** ★ Overhanging face.
5. **Wet Sex B1-** ★

Giant Rock
Map 2
1. **Cement Arête 5.10** ★

JOSHUA TREE

Joshua Tree is home to the most expansive and difficult bouldering in California. The ratings are characteristic of Joshua Tree, and many problems may seem underrated to the newcomer. Boulders seem to cover the landscape at Joshua Tree but, fortunately for this guide, the good bouldering is all concentrated in small areas. The best bouldering will be found at **Hidden Valley Campground, Turtle Rock, Gunsmoke, Cap Rock**, and the **Asteroid Belt**. The rock is a very coarse quartz monzonite that quickly wears down tender fingers and rubber soles if your footwork is less than optimum. Roped climbing is the primary attraction of Joshua Tree. Randy Vogel's *Joshua Tree Rock Climbing Guide* gives a full description of routes and amenities. For additional detailed bouldering information, see Mari Gingery's *Joshua Tree Bouldering Guide.*

Though quality roped routes are plentiful, most climbers take time to explore the vast amounts of bouldering during their stay. And since some of the best climbers in the world have enjoyed extended stays at Joshua Tree, the area has produced some of the hardest boulder problems in Southern California.

Historically, little is known of the early bouldering development by Royal Robbins and his cohorts during the late fifties and early sixties. During the late sixties however, the "Desert Rats," which included John Wolfe, Bob Dominick, "Speedy" Gonzalez and Dick Webster, developed many problems in the campground vicinity, including the **Triangle** and **Intersection Boulders**. The first Joshua Tree guide, authored by John Wolfe, contained a bouldering section with a description of about 20 problems ranging from 5.6 to 5.9 (several of these are considered 5.10 now).

In the early seventies, John Long was the first to make a concentrated effort at seeking out difficult boulder problems. With his extremely powerful climbing ability, many of his problems were characterized by off-the-deck moves and huge dynos. **The White Rastafarian** (5.11+R) is the best-known of his problems. John Bachar arrived soon after and began developing entirely new areas: **The JBMFP, Turtle Rock, Gunsmoke, and Planet X**. He was probably the best boulderer of this era, and many of his problems remained unrepeated for a number of years. His ability to climb difficult moves well off the deck led to higher and higher problems that may well go beyond the normal definition of bouldering. Many of these problems are now top-roped by most climbers, but are given a fall factor of X, since he initially climbed many of them unroped. Mike Lechlinski, Mari Gingery, John Yablonski, Mike Paul, Jerry Moffat, Skip Guerin, Craig Fry, Kevin Powell, Dick Cilley, Darrel Hensel, Russ Walling and Roy McClenahan were also very active in establishing new areas and problems from the late seventies into the early nineties.

Camping at Hidden Valley has become increasingly more difficult as Joshua Tree becomes more popular each year. Primitive camping (of questionable legality) can be found outside the Monument boundaries. An entrance fee is charged to enter the Monument. Most climbers get a Golden Eagle Pass for unlimited access.

Season: Joshua Tree is at an elevation of over 4,000 feet, with the best weather beginning in October and lasting through May. Mid-winter is usually good, but high wind conditions boost the chill factor, causing even the most hardy climbers to keep their hands in their pockets.

1

2

Sequence of Boone Speed on Planet X (B2 ★ R) at Joshua Tree.

3

Joshua Tree Overview Map (pages 126-127)

A. Quail Springs Picnic Area

Whipper 5.11+ Thin face just right of the wide crack on the SE face.

Ripper 5.11 Lieback left of Wallaby Crack on NE face.

Gripper Traverse 5.10 Traverse from Ripper to Butterfly crack, NE face.

B. AFPA Across From Picnic Area Rock.

Hand Crack 5.8 Crack on boulder in front of AFPA Rock.

Stahl Arête 5.10 Arête to the right of the hand crack.

C. Broken Boulders

Blort 5.11+ ★ Arête NE corner, east boulder.

Church of The Jack Lord 5.10 R North face of west boulder.

Bubblebutt B1- Left side of west face, west boulder. Cheatstone.

Sidestep 5.10+ Step off boulder onto face; right side, west face.

Crack 5.6 Southwest face.

D. Soviet Block Boulder

Two problems are on boulder at the base of Soviet Block.

E. Bardini Crack 5.11 ★ Overhanging lieback crack.

F. S-Crack Area, Yabo Boulder

Yabaho B1 Northeast face.

Dinkey Doinks 5.11 Northwest face.

G. Jimmy Cliff

Penguins in Bondage B1 R Many problems in area.

H. Sports Challenge Rock

Lobster Lieback B1+ Lieback just right of "Dick Emberg" Tree.

Kirkatron 5.11+/B1 Traverse from Lobster Lieback to Championship Wrestling.

I. Slash Boulder

On the approach to The Equinox. Many problems exist in this area and in the Virgin Isles Area.

Slash Face 5.11+ ★ OTD Steep boulder with many horizontal slashes.

Seam Splitter B1 Seam on north face, cheatstone.

J. Jumbo Rock Boulder Face

Several good problems on face with quality rock facing road just down from the Jumbo Rock campground entrance.

K. Big Bob's Big Wedge B1

Thirty-foot hand and fist roof-crack with a sit-down start, approach from east parking cul-de-sac at Live Oak Picnic Area and hike 300 yards SW to large boulder on hillside.

Johnny Woodward flashing "All Washed Up" (B1 R), Cup Rock Area.

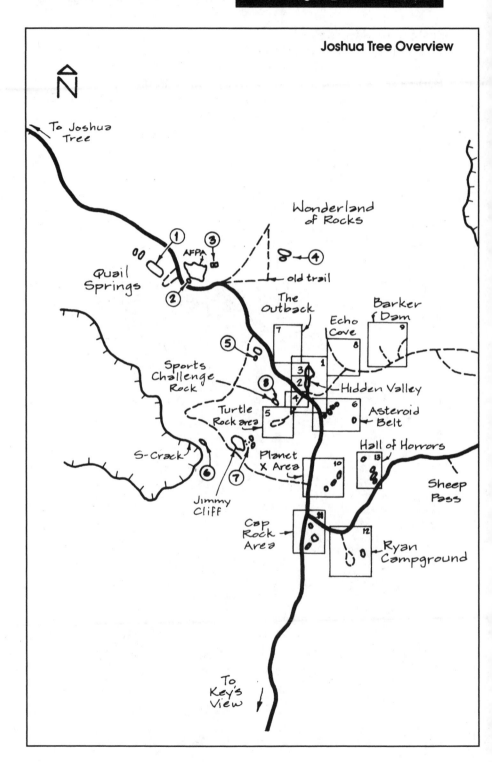

Joshua Tree Overview

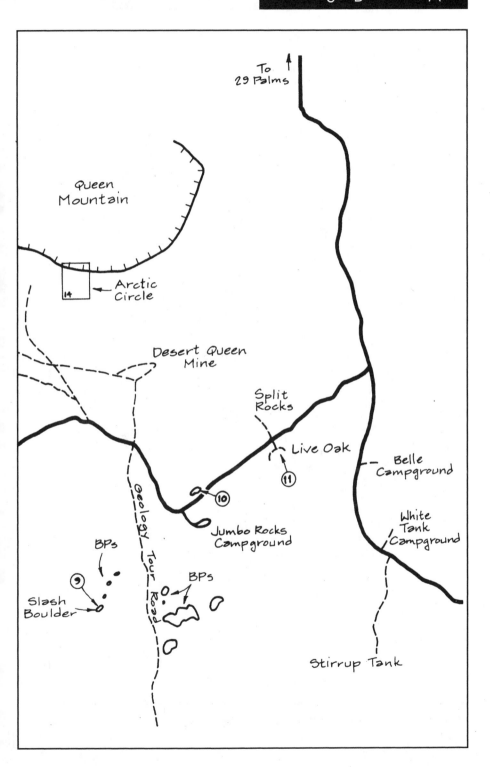

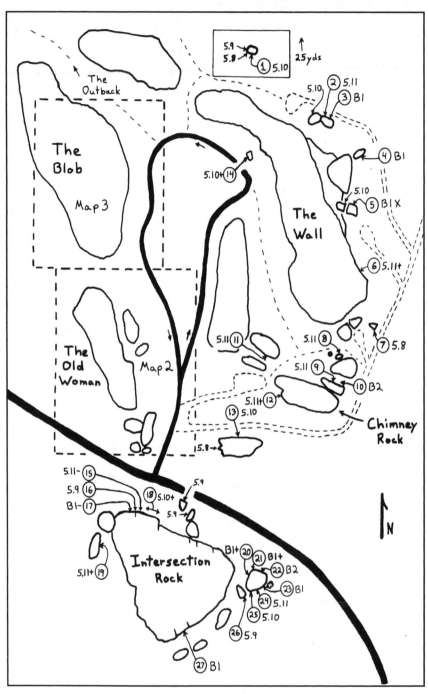

Joshua Tree, Hidden Valley Campground
Map 1

Joshua Tree, Hidden Valley Campground
Map 1

1. **Pinhead 5.10** ★ Pin-scarred thin seam.
2. **Lemon 5.11** Scoop problem.
3. **Orange Julius B1+** Vertical orange dike.
4. **Fire'e or Retire'e B1** Friction.
5. **Having Fun Yet? B1** X Face.
6. **The Upside Down Pineapple 5.11+** Slanting roof crack.
7. **Phallus 5.8** Left arête is **5.9**.
8. **Weenie Roast 5.11**
9. **Rats with Wings 5.11** ★ Crack.
10. **Guerin Traverse B2** Seam traverse.
11. **Lunar Lieback 5.11-**
12. **Copper Penny 5.11+** R
13. **Pothole Problem 5.10**
14. **The Blank 5.10** R
15. **Augie Problem 5.11-**
16. **Knuckle Cracker 5.9** Flared crack.
17. **Rieder Problem B1-** ★
18. **Intersection Rock Traverse 5.10+** ★ Right to left.
19. **The Punk 5.11+** X
20. **Anglo Saxophone B1+** Without cheatstone **B2**.
21. **Sweetspot B1+**
22. **Mediterranean Sundance B2** Very long reach required, or run and jump.
23. **Intersection Boulder Right B1-**
24. **Intersection Boulder Center 5.11** ★
25. **Intersection Boulder Left 5.10** ★
26. **Intersection Mantel 5.9**
27. **Moon Lieback B1** Cheatstone.

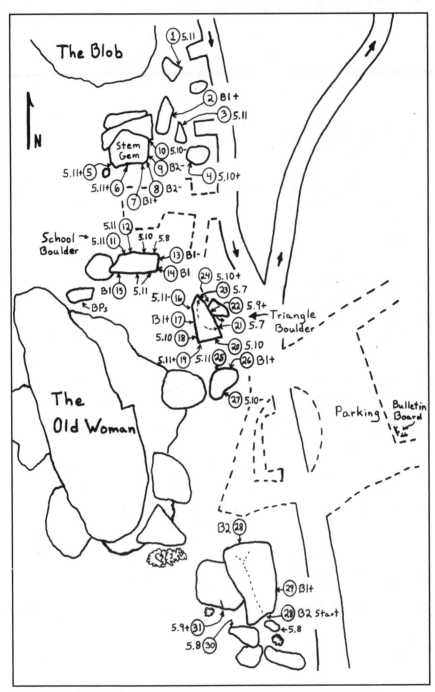

Joshua Tree Map, Hidden Valley Campground
Map 2

Joshua Tree Map, Hidden Valley Campground Map 2

1. **Boondoggle 5.11**
2. **Yabolator B1+** Work up and left through scoops.
3. **The Totem 5.11** Elimination problem on left side of arête.
4. **Sloperfest 5.10+**
5. **Slam Dunk 5.11+** Jump for scoop and mantle.
6. **Stem Gem 5.11+/B1-** ★ Stem up and right on to friction face.
7. **Stem Gem Mantel B1+**
8. **Vice Grip B2**
9. **Rump Seam B2**
10. **Piss Crack 5.10-** Overhanging hand crack.
11. **Junior Varsity Mantel 5.11**
12. **Varsity Crank Problem 5.11** ★
13. **Cheese Grater B1-**
14. **Largonaut B1** ★
15. **Mumbles Mumblephone B1**
16. **Dynamo Hum 5.11-** ★ Many variations.
17. **Triangle Face Center B1+**
18. **Old Triangle Classic 5.10** ★
19. **Century Bell 5.11+**
20. **South Face 5.10**
21. **South Side Descent 5.7** Descent route.
22. **East Face Direct 5.9**
23. **North Side Descent 5.7** Descent route.
24. **Easter Bunny Back Scrapper 5.10+** Low traverse through cave.
25. **Roundup 5.11** Mantel.
26. **Basketball Jump B1+/J1+** Jump for dish and mantel.
27. **Press Test 5.10** Mantel.
28. **Caveman B2** Hueco traverse from south to north. From north to south B2+.
29. **Cashbox B1+/J1+** Jump for scoop.
30. **Split Grain 5.8** Arête.
31. **Bushwhack 5.9+** Lieback flared crack.

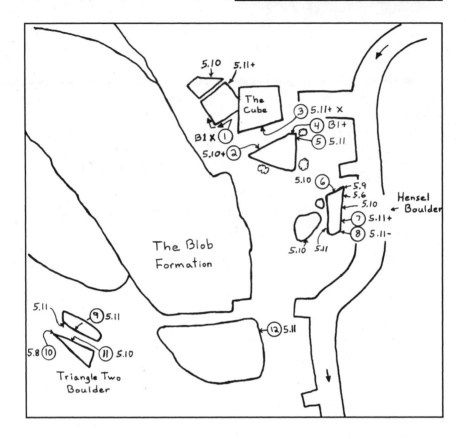

Joshua Tree, Hidden Valley Campground
Map 3
1. **Bachar's Traverse B1** X
2. **Lapse of Logic 5.10+**
3. **The Funktion 5.11+** X Cheatstone.
4. **Scatterbrain B1+** ★
5. **Bard's Ankle 5.11** ★ R Bad landing potential.
6. **Scoop Problem 5.10**
7. **Hensel Face 5.11+**
8. **Hensel Arête 5.11-** ★
9. **Black Pea 5.11**
10. **Triangle Two Arête 5.8** Descent route.
11. **Triangle Two Face 5.10** One start, many upper variations.
12. **Tex Mex 5.11** Crack to hole.

Joshua Tree: JBMFP
(John Bachar Memorial Face Problem) Area
Map 4
1. **English Leather 5.11** OTD
2. **The Terminator B1** OTD
2a. **Skip's Arête B1+**
3. **Lechlinski's Corner 5.11+** ★ Arête.
4. **Hensel Face 5.11+**
5. **Razarium B1** ★ AKA: Easy JBMFP.
6. **JBMFP B1+** ★ Steep thin face.
7. **Ture Grit 5.11+** ★ Traverse arête.
8. **The False Up 20 5.9+** ★ Lieback.
9. **Splatter Proof 5.10** OTD
10. **Shindig 5.11** ★ Face to curving crack.
11. **False Blockhead 5.11+** ★
12. **Yabo Roof 5.11+** Yabo start to roof traverse.
13. **Yardarm 5.11**

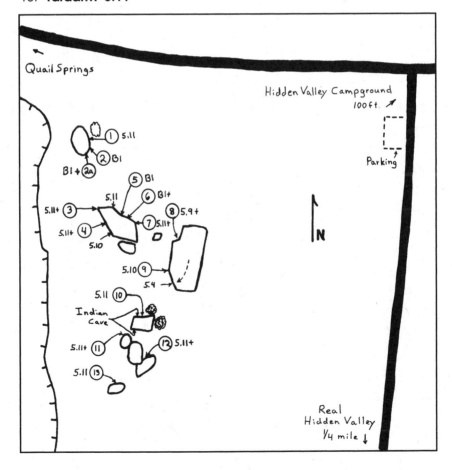

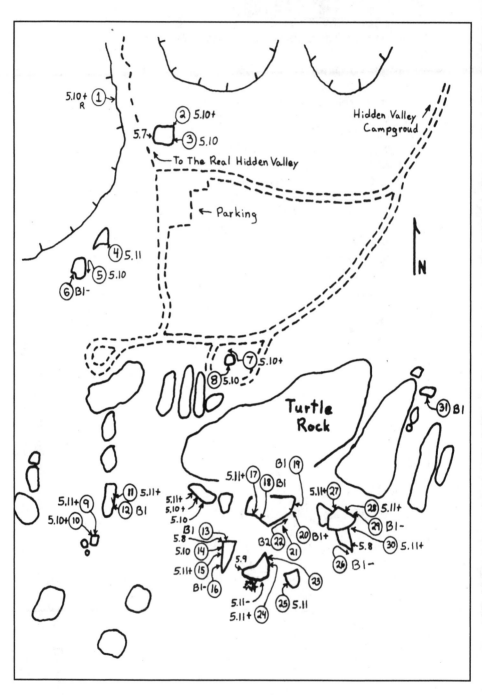

Joshua Tree, Real Hidden Valley and Turtle Rock
Map 5

Joshua Tree, Real Hidden Valley and Turtle Rock
Map 5

1. **Betty Jo Yablonski 5.10+ ★** R Steep horizontal cracks to vertical crack lieback.
2. **Stand Up for Your Rights 5.10+**
3. **Sign Problem 5.10**
4. **Soft Pretzel 5.11**
†5. **Night Crawler 5.10** Friction traverse.
†6. **Saturday Night Live B1-** Full flying dyno.
†7. **Creeping Jew 5.10+** Full boulder traverse, no hands at low section near tree.
†8. **Sprinting Jew 5.10** Run up slab.
9. **Black Velvet 5.11+**
10. **Classic Curl 5.10+ ★**
11. **Yawning Flare 5.11+** Right and left.
12. **Jump Chump B1/J1** Run and jump for high hold.
13. **Blood Mantel B1**
14. **Turtle Face Left 5.10 ★**
15. **Turtle Face Center 5.11+** OTD
16. **Turtle Knob B1- ★**
17. **Sorta High 5.11+** R
18. **Button High B1 ★** R
19. **Crank City B1 ★** R Right hand start to So High, jump off to escape.
20. **So High B1+ ★** X Overhanging crack/face to flaring exit.
21. **Boiler Plates** Overhanging plates, does not go to top.
22. **Powerband West B2** Sit-down start at left end, traverse right to jug on So High.
23. **Wave Arête. Right Side 5.8** Arête. **Center B1. Left Side 5.11+.** Rounded arête just right of Accomazzo Face.
24. **Accomazzo Face 5.11+** Friction.
25. **Turnbuckle 5.11** Undercling to funky mantle.
26. **Shipwreck Arête B1-** R Traverse.
27. **Block Party 5.11+** Undercut flake.
28. **Turboflange 5.11+** Center face.
29. **Neoflange B1-** Overhanging arête.
30. **Fist Full of Walnuts 5.11+ ★** Overhanging crack formed by two boulders.
31. **Egghead B1** Steep crank.

†   *These problems are commonly done at night.*

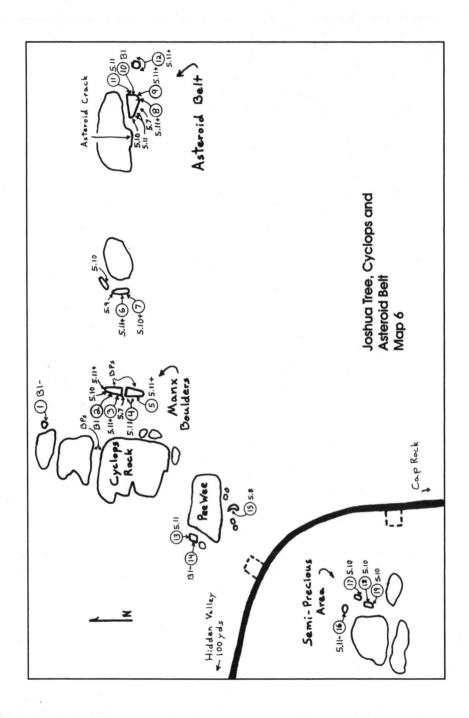

Joshua Tree, Cyclops and
Asteroid Belt
Map 6

Joshua Tree, Cyclops and Asteroid Belt
Map 6
1. **Pig Pen   B1-** AKA: Bachar Cracker of the Desert. Roof crack. with cave start.
2. **Off Camber B1** Mantle or dyno from sloping shelf.
3. **Out of Touch 5.11+** Undercling to sloper summit mantle.
4. **Fish Bait 5.11-** Left route.
   Xylophone 5.11 Center route.
   The Boxer Problem 5.11 Right route.
5. **Undertow 5.11+ ★** Work from seam up and left.
6. **The Smoke Detector 5.11+** Undercling to face.
7. **Burning Sensation 5.10+** Grainy face.
8. **Pea Brain 5.11+ ★** Lieback thin crack.
9. **Optigrip 5.11+ ★** Start with left hand in Pea Brain crack and move into right crack.
10. **Underdog B1** Two variations with undercut bottom.
11. **Face Off 5.11** Face with small black knobs.
12. **The Orbiter 5.11+** Traverse around entire boulder.
13. **Key Largo 5.11 ★** Work up and left from center jug.
14. **Chip Flakey B1-** Undercling lieback flake.
15. **The Womb 5.8** Climb up and left out of scoop.
16. **Zinger 5.11-**
17. **Belly Roll 5.10**
18. **Hot and Juicy 5.10** Thin crack to sloper summit.
19. **Semi-Precious 5.10 ★** AKA: The Poor Man's Stem Gem.

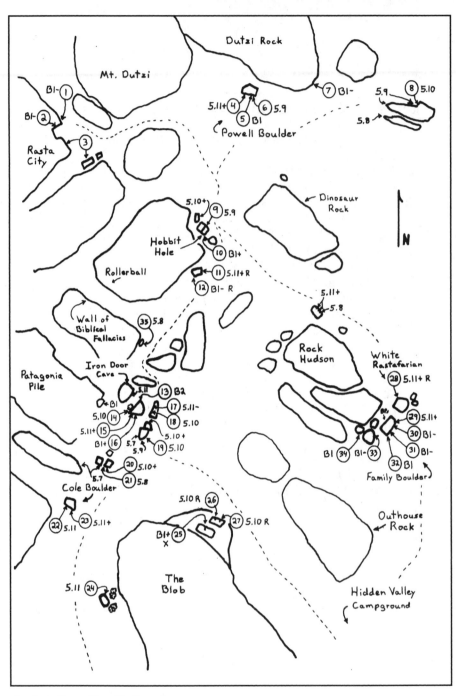

Joshua Tree, The Outback
Map 7

Joshua Tree, The Outback
Map 7

1. **Scorpion Traverse B1-** Cave start to crack.
   Viragoron Variation B1; start at Scorpion first hold and climb up to horizontal.
2. **Digitations B1-** Seam.
3. **Rasta City** Many short cracks and knobby faces.
4. **Powell Face 5.11+** ★
5. **Largo Dyno B1** Dyno off left-side of sloping shelf.
6. **Largotot 5.9** Reach off right-side of sloping shelf.
7. **Jimmy The Weasel B1-** Face with two discontinuous seams.
8. **Coyote Corner 5.10** OTD Jugs on left-side of corner.
9. **Hobbit Offwidth 5.9** Offwidth or lieback.
10. **Animal B1+** ★ Arête.
11. **Friction Addiction 5.11+** R
12. **Moon Germs B1-** R Cheatstone to mantel.
13. **Tidal Wave (Rating unknown.)** Arête.
14. **Bedrock Arête 5.10** ★ Fight pine tree to climb left side of arête.
15. **Stoney Point Problem 5.11+**
16. **Yabba-Dabba-Doo B1+** Dyno.
17. **Chuckawalla 5.11-** ★ Lieback start, many variations.
18. **Flintlock Dyno 5.10** ★ Many variations.
19. **Dino Egg 5.10** ★
20. **Scissor Lock 5.10+**
21. **Voice's Arête 5.9**
22. **Cole Dihedral 5.11**
23. **Cole Arête 5.11+** ★ Cheatstone.
24. **Laura Scudder 5.11** Scoops to loose flakes.
25. **Central Scrutinizer B1+** X Thin crack, usually top-roped.
26. **Left Nixon Crack 5.10** ★ R
27. **Right Nixon Crack 5.10** ★ R
28. **White Rastafarian 5.11+** ★ R
29. **Little Sister 5.11+**
30. **How's Your Grandma B1-**
31. **How's Your Mama B1-** ★
32. **How's Your Papa B1** ★ Arête.
33. **Bamboozler B1-**
34. **The Jerk B1** R
35. **Mr. Crack 5.8** ★

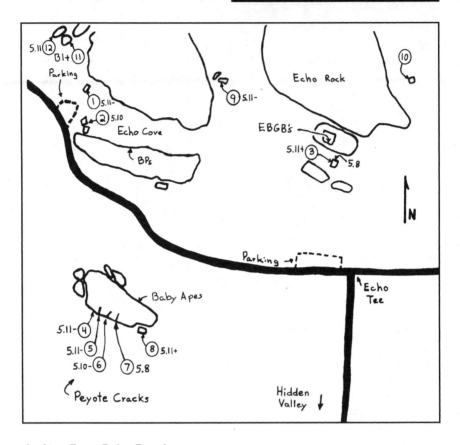

Joshua Tree, Echo Tee Area
Map 8

1. **Echo Cove Thin Crack 5.11-** ★
2. **Arête Boulders 5.9 to 5.10+** Many problems.
3. **Flake Dyno 5.11+** OTD
4. **Matt's Pinch 5.11-** ★
5. **Left Peyote Crack 5.11-** ★ Easy climbing above crux.
6. **Center Peyote Crack 5.10** Easy climbing above crux.
7. **Right Peyote Crack 5.8** Route.
8. **Yabble Babble 5.11+**
9. **Steam Train 5.11** ★ Dike traverse.
10. **Gumdrop Boulder** Many problems.
11. **Igneous Ambiance B1+** ★ Sit-down start in cave.
12. **Grungy Arête 5.11**

Joshua Tree, Barker Dam Area
Map 9

1. **Piano Rock Crack 5.9**
2. **Retrofit 5.10** Many more problems have been done on Piano Rock.
3. **The Tube 5.10+** OTD Thin arch leads to mantle over yucca plants.
4. **High Noon B1** R Seam above traverse.
5. **Corner Problem 5.10+**
6. **Gunsmoke 5.11** ★ Traverse.
7. **Streetcar Named Desire B2-** ★ Stem, or run and mantle.
8. **Petroglyph 5.11+** Crack problem to undercling. Upper section is 5.9 X.
9. **Mr. Coffee 5.11+** Lieback flake.
10. **Liquid Wrench 5.10+** Traverse flake.
11. **Chicken Wing 5.9**
12. **Crack 5.10+** TR Boost to start. Bottom section has not yet been freed.
13. **Old Wave 5.11** ★
14. **New Wave B1** ★
15. **Big Kahuna 5.10+** TR

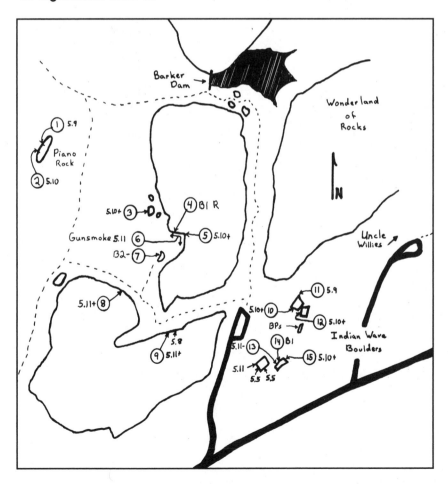

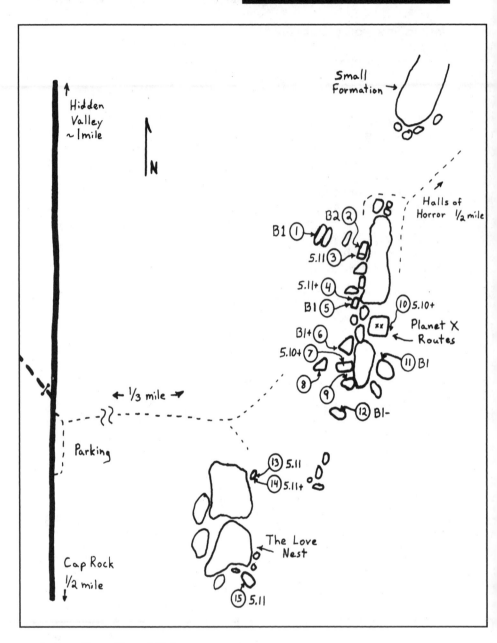

Small Formation →

↑
Hidden
Valley
~ 1 mile

↑
N

Halls of
Horror ½ mile

B2 ②
B1 ①

5.11 ③

5.11+ ④

B1 ⑤

⑩ 5.10+
XX
Planet X
Routes

B1+ ⑥

5.10+ ⑦

⑪ B1

⑧

⑨

⑫ B1-

← ⅓ mile →

Parking

⑬ 5.11
⑭ 5.11+

The Love
Nest

Cap Rock
½ mile
↓

⑮ 5.11

Joshua Tree, Planet X Area
Map 10

Joshua Tree, Planet X Area
Map 10
1. **Jerry's Kids B1** ★
2. **Planet X B2 R** ★ Descend wide crack--**The Wormhole 5.10.**
3. **Lucky Star 5.11** R
4. **Satellite Boulder Left Side 5.11+** ★ OTD
5. **Satellite Boulder Right Side B1** R
6. **Schooly Penis B1+** Cheatstone
7. **Boulder Crack 5.10+** ★
8. **Unknown** Has not been completed.
9. **OK Face 5.8** Center of face.
9a. **Alright Arete 5.9** Right arete.
10. **Planet Traverse 5.10+** Traverse right to left.
11. **Turbolator B1** Cheatstone.
12. **Newton's Law B1-**
13. **Mahogany 5.11**
14. **Woody Problem 5.11+**
15. **Snakecharmer 5.11** OTD

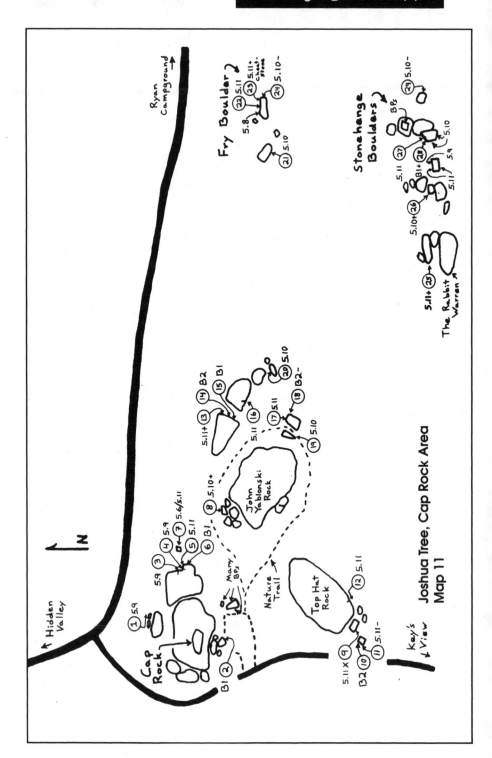

Joshua Tree, Cap Rock Area
Map 11

Joshua Tree, Cap Rock Area
Map 11
1. **Graham Parsons Memorial Hand Traverse 5.9**
2. **Parking Lot Problem B1** Overhanging seam.
3. **Short Crack 5.9**
4. **White Crack 5.9** ★
5. **Love Handle 5.11** Face.
6. **High Heeled Sneakers B1** OTD
7. **Four Corners Boulder: North 5.6, West 5.11, South 5.10, East 5.10+**
8. **Collieherb 5.10+** ★ Horizontal slashes.
9. **Up 40 5.11** X Lieback. Can be led; for solo descent—jump across chasm.
10. **Powell Crank B2** Arête.
11. **Powell Pinch 5.11** Left-sloping arête.
12. **Traverse to 1¼" Crack 5.11**
13. **All Lunged Out 5.11** ★ Traverse left to dyno move.
14. **Soar Eagle B2** Center face.
15. **All Washed Up B1** ★ R Left side of face; sloper finish.
16. **Up 20 5.11** R Flared, wide crack lieback.
17. **Largo Dyno 5.11** Jump for dish and mantel.
18. **Pumping Monzonite B2** ★
19. **South Arête 5.10** ★
20. **The False Ayatollah 5.10** ★
21. **Reach for a Peach 5.10** Descend route.
22. **Fry Problem 5.11** ★ Overhanging face.
23. **Leap in Faith 5.11+** Extra large cheatstone or jump is required to reach first holds.
24. **Compone 5.10-**
25. **Sand Castle 5.11+** R Flared cracks up arête.
26. **Picture Perfect 5.10+** ★ Overhanging arête.
27. **Foot Fetish 5.11** ★ OTD
28. **Prince Fari B1+** Elimination problem on left side of arête.
29. **Mushroom Boulder 5.10-** Descend route.

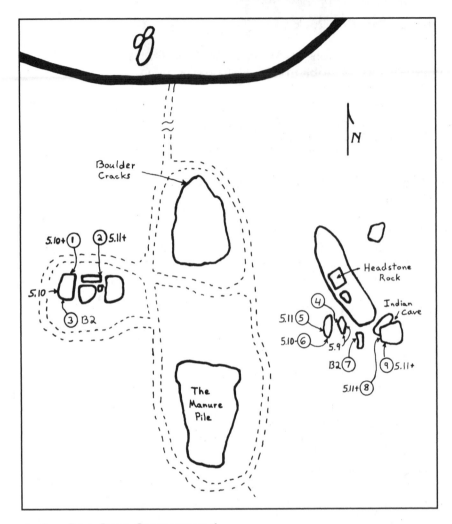

Joshua Tree, Ryan Campground
Map 12
1. **Gibb Arête 5.10+**
2. **Flight Attendant 5.11+/B1- ★** Arête.
3. **Dreaming of the Master B2**
4. **Facet Cut (Rating Unknown.)** Right side of arête.
5. **Figure Five 5.11 ★** Slashes.
6. **Fidelman Arête 5.10-**
7. **Chili Sauce B2 ★** aka Moffat Problem.
8. **Metate Face 5.11+ ★** OTD
9. **Stab in the Dark 5.11+**

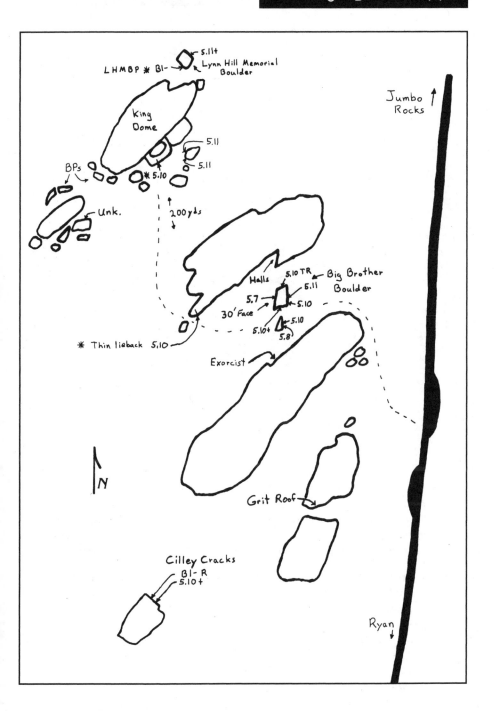

Joshua Tree, Hall of Horrors Bouldering
Map 13

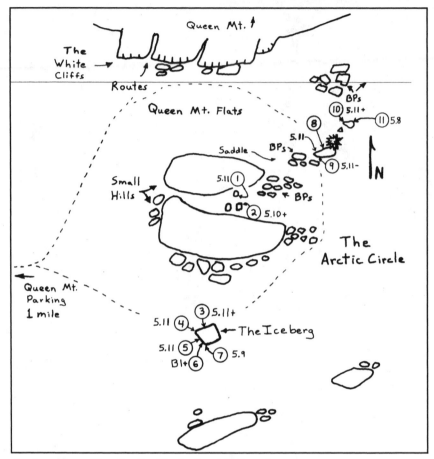

Joshua Tree, The Arctic Circle Bouldering Area
Map 14

Approach from Queen Mountain parking area. Hike approximately 1.0 mile due east—no trail—and head for dark rock boulderfield to the right of the Queen Mountain Flats Cliff band.

1. **Undertaker 5.11** Overhanging bulge with flared crack above.
2. **Bounty Hunter Arête 5.10+** ★
3. **Belt Sander 5.11+**
4. **Frozen Razor 5.11**
5. **Remote Sensor 5.11** ★ Cheatstone.
6. **Golden Mary B1+/B2**
7. **Binding Arête 5.9** R
8. **Anti-Matter** ★ (Rating Unknown.)
9. **The Bull Horn 5.11-**
10. **Todd's Problem 5.11+** Long reaches between holes.
11. **Spiral Staircase 5.8** Descent.

The hills of Riverside County are covered with boulders. These hills extend through San Diego County and into Mexico, and the bouldering possibilities are virtually endless.

Riverside County Areas

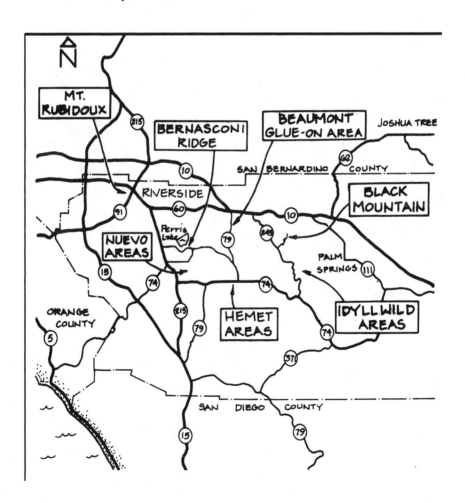

MOUNT RUBIDOUX

Mount Rubidoux is perhaps the most popular bouldering area in
Riverside County. Rubidoux is a large boulder-covered hill that is
now a city park with a very narrow, winding road that leads to its
cross-topped summit. Though the area is known primarily as a
beginners' area, Rubidoux has a brilliant array of quality boulder
problems and top-rope routes. Beginners will find that **Joe Brown**,
Half Dome, and **Cross Rock** are excellent areas to practice technique
and rope skills. Advanced climbers can complete huge circuits of
quality problems and top-ropes. The rock is light-colored quartz
monzonite and has a relatively smooth texture.

Steve Mackey compiled the first xerox guide in 1976. It contained one
map and gave a full paragraph description for every known problem
on the hill at the time. His intentions were good, but the guide was

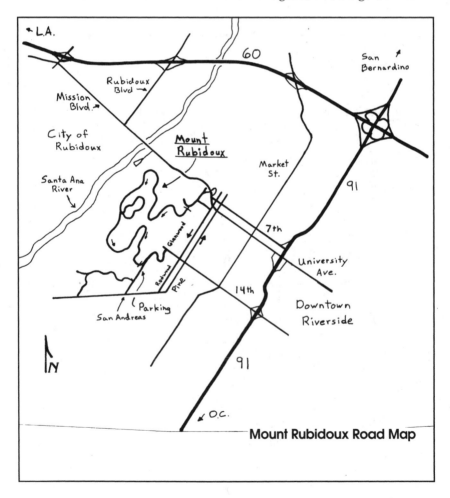

Mount Rubidoux Road Map

never popular. In 1983 and 1984, Randy Vogel organized bouldering contests here, and with the help of Kevin Powell and Darrel Hensel encouraged a new enthusiasm for Rubidoux. The maps that served as a guide for the bouldering contests became underground guides of a sort. Mt. Rubidoux has more names for boulder problems than anywhere else. This naming tradition started with Steve Mackey's guidebook, but many were renamed by Randy Vogel, Kevin Powell, and Darrel Hensel and documented in the bouldering contest maps.

Long before it became known for good rock climbing, Mt. Rubidoux had already earned a niche in the history of Riverside County. This 500-foot hill was part of an original Spanish land grant that became a favorite hiking area and respite for the late Frank A. Miller. Miller was the owner and founder of the now historic Mission Inn in Riverside when, in 1905, he and two friends organized a park association aimed at purchasing the mountain and developing it as a park for the residents of Riverside. Two months after Miller succeeded in having the area recognized as a park, he had a large cross erected on its highest point, dedicated to Father Junipero Serra, with a bronze plaque personally unveiled by President Taft. Two years after the cross was erected, the first of many historic Easter Sunrise Services was held. The first service in 1908 had 100 participants, a number that has grown to over 20,000 in recent years.

Little is known of the first climbers to frequent Mt. Rubidoux. In the late sixties and early seventies its popularity increased as serious attention was given to Rubidoux by Phil Haney and Paul Gleason. Soon after, some local boys from the Upland area learned to climb there. John Long, Rick Accomazzo, Richard Harrison, Rob Muir, and Tobin Sorenson were among the most prominent of these lads, and later went on to form the core of the "Stonemasters." An early prerequisite to becoming a Stonemaster was leading the Valhalla route at **Suicide Rock**, Southern California's first 5.11. The Stonemasters became excellent boulderers and dominated the local scene with new development. As the Stonemasters eventually went on to new crags, Kevin Powell and Darrel Hensel took up the slack. Known as "dime-cranking masters," these two found many new desperates.

The road up Mt. Rubidoux is closed because portions of the roadbed have washed away in storms. Most climbers park on San Andreas at the bottom of the hill and walk up. Poison oak is rampant on the north slopes.

The best time to climb at Mt. Rubidoux is fall through spring. Riverside tends to get very hot and smoggy during the summer, although good climbing can be done in the evenings.

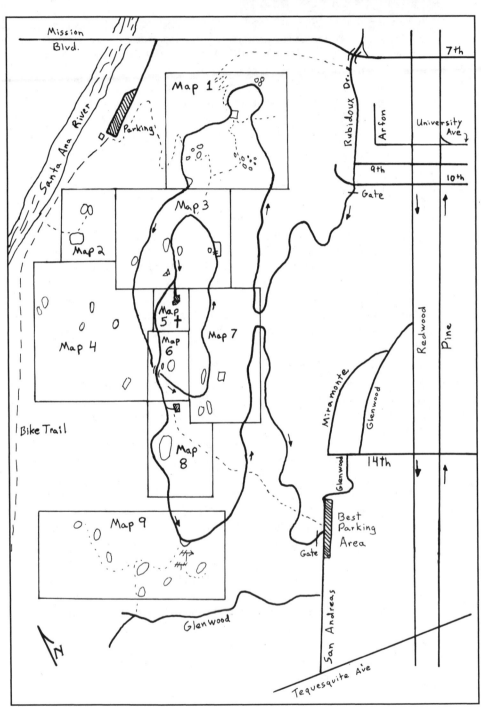

Mount Rubidoux Overview

Mount Rubidoux Map Key:

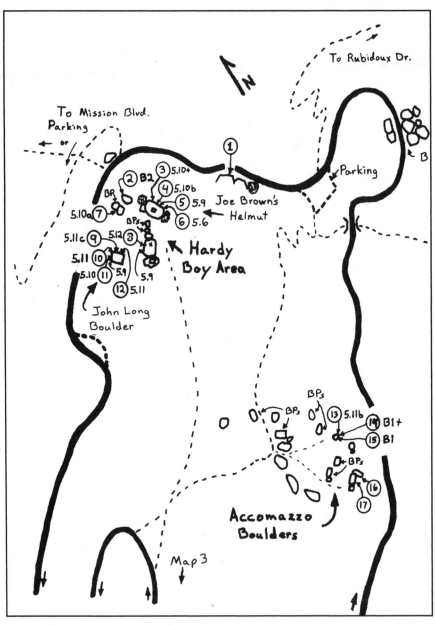

**Rubidoux, Hardy Boy Area and Accomazzo Boulders
Map 1**

Rubidoux, Hardy Boy Area and Accomazzo Boulders
Map 1
1. **Peppertree Arête 5.9 to 5.11** Several boulder problems.
2. **The Octopus B2** Arête.
3. **Joe Brown's Helmet 5.10+** TR
4. **Joe Brown's Dimp 5.10b** ★ TR
5. **Little Brown Jug 5.9** TR
6. **Super Moth 5.6**
7. **The Fu Crack 5.10a** ★ Overhanging crack.
8. **The Hardy Boy Crack 5.12** ★ TR Pin-scarred seam.
9. **J. Elvis 5.11c**
10. **Momma's in New York 5.11** ★ Arête.
11. **The Big Guy 5.10**
12. **The Runaway 5.11**
13. **Spitfire 5.11b**
14. **High Brow B1**
15. **Bullet Head B1**
16. Boulder problems, from left to right:
    The Hand That Takes 5.11a Left side.
    Face Lift B2- Center face.
    Street Corner 5.10a Left side of arête.
    The Bum 5.11a Center of arête.
    Back Alley 5.10a Right side of arête.
17. Boulder problems, from left to right:
    Over Your Head 5.11c TR Left of offwidth.
    High Water 5.9 Offwidth crack.
    Run For It 5.10d Right of the offwidth.

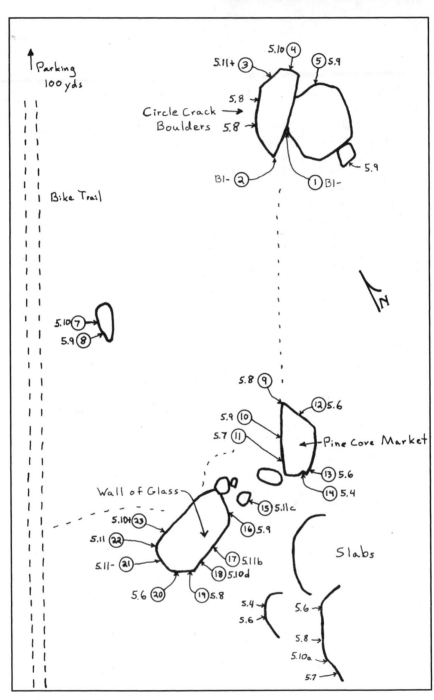

Rubidoux, Wall of Glass Area
Map 2

Rubidoux, Wall of Glass Area
Map 2
Approach from Mission Blvd. parking area.
1. **Circle Crack B1-** ★ Overhanging crack.
2. **Circle Crack Arête B1-**
3. **Don't Touch Me There 5.11+**
4. **Hug Me 5.10**
5. **D.C. 5.9**
7. **Cheri's Face 5.10**
8. **Cheri's Arm 5.9**
9. **Lou 5.8** Arête.
10. **The Warning 5.9**
11. **Peggy 5.7**
12. **The Brain 5.6**
13. **Clark 5.6**
14. **Pine Cove Market 5.4** Start off block to gain upper ledge.
15. **Roll up the Window 5.11c** Mantel.
16. **Windex 5.9**
17. **Surrealistic Pillar 5.11b** ★
18. **Window Pane 5.10d**
19. **Punch Bowl Right 5.8**
20. **Punch Bowl Left 5.6**
21. **Contest Giveaway 5.11-** Run and mantel.
22. **Suction Cup 5.11** Mantel.
23. **Plexiglass 5.10+**

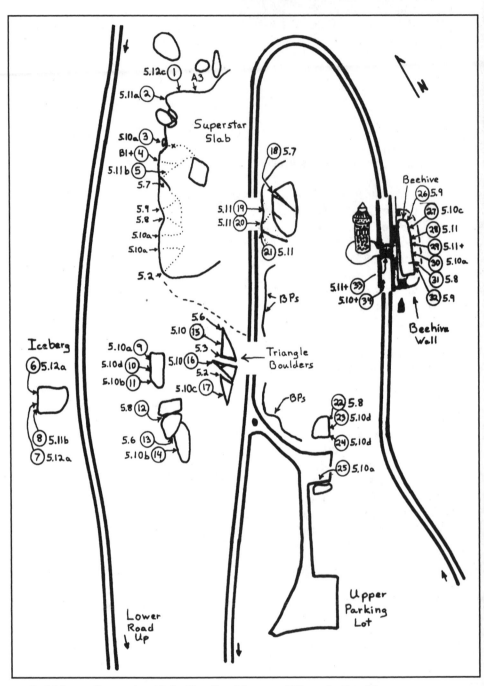

**Rubidoux: Superstar Slab, The Beehive and Triangle Boulders
Map 3**

Rubidoux: Superstar Slab, The Beehive and Triangle Boulders Map 3

1. **Coathanger 5.12c** Friction; lead or top-rope.
2. **Frosty Cone 5.11a** TR
3. **Superstar 5.10a** Bolted lead.
4. **Flabob B1+** Black streak.
5. **Side of Fries 5.11b** ★ Face.
6. **Snow Blind 5.12a** TR
7. **Frost Bite 5.12a** TR
8. **The Big Stick 5.11b** Boost to start.
9. **Aggravation 5.10a**
10. **Overfilled Water Bed 5.10d**
11. **Drunk at the Wedding 5.10b**
12. **The Folly Left 5.8** Wide crack.
13. **The Folly Right 5.6**
14. **Horizontal Bands 5.10b**
15. **Triangle Face 5.10** ★ Many variations.
16. **Isosceles 5.10** TR
17. **Triangulation 5.10c**
18. **Holiday in Berlin 5.7** Wide crack.
19. **Muir Trail 5.11**
20. **Haney Overhang 5.11** TR Face to overhanging thin crack.
21. **Beach Problem 5.11** ★ Yabo start to arête, exit right.
22. **Boy Scout Mantel 5.8**
23. **Tenderfoot 5.10d**
24. **Bat Flake 5.10d**
25. **Arm Pit Mantel 5.10a**
26. **Beehive Lieback 5.9**
27. **Beehive Mantel 5.10c**
28. **Bumble Bee 5.11** ★ Face up and right.
29. **Killer Bees 5.11+** Face up and right.
30. **King Bee 5.10**
31. **Beehive Crack 5.8** ★
32. **Honey Combs 5.9** Face at left end of wall.
33. **Peace Bridge 5.11** Both sides. Traverse the bridge without using the top.
34. **Wall Traverse 5.10+**

Rubidoux, Half Moon Area
Map 4
1. **Laughing Cow Crack 5.7**
2. **Clarifloculator 5.10** TR Face.
3. **Underflow 5.10+** TR Face.
4. **Ungelating Mass 5.11** TR
5. **Stack Sample 5.9**
6. **Poison Oak Face 5.10** TR
7. **Green 5.10a** ★
8. **Gold 5.10a**
9. **Koh-i-noor 5.8** ★
10. **Half Moon Crack 5.10d** Wide crack.
11. **Full Moon 5.10c**
12. **Clinker 5.10**
13. **Wilson Overhang 5.11**
14. **Baghouse 5.9** Offwidth.
15. **Fly Ash 5.10**
16. **Turtle Dome Crack 5.10b** ★ Hand or B1 Lieback.
17. **Mrs. Reagan 5.10c**
18. **Mama Mantel 5.11**
19. **Tiny Hole Mantel 5.10b**
20. **The Mug B1+**
21. **Crank like a Cancer 5.10d**
22. **Thumbellina 5.10a** ★
23. **Cherry Dip Scoop 5.10b**
24. **Palsey 5.11c** TR
25. **Spaz Attack 5.11a** TR
26. **The Cheater Overhang 5.9** Yabo start B1
27. **Rob's Problem B1** TR

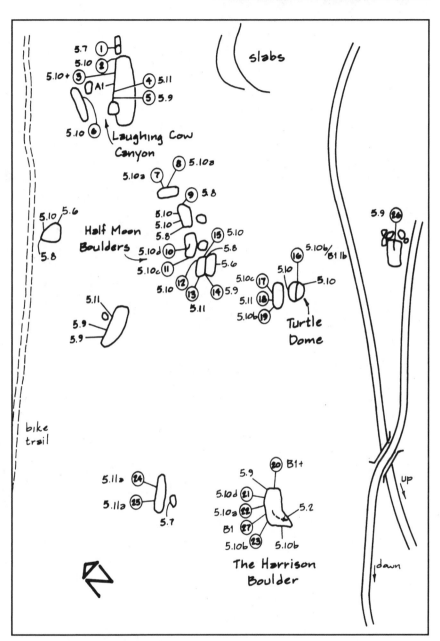

Rubidoux, Half Moon Area
Map 4

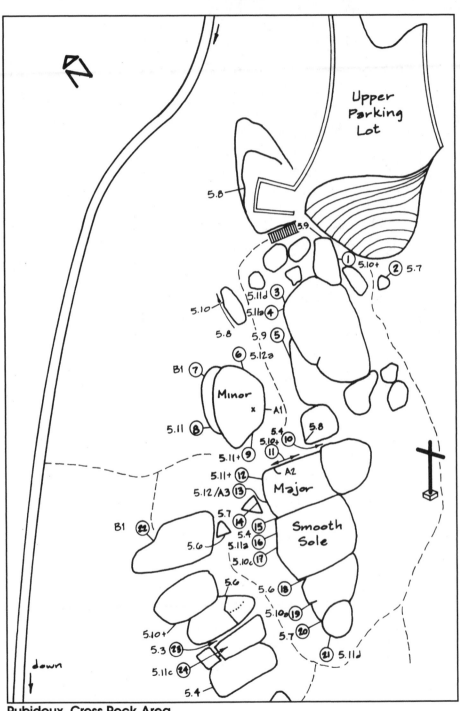

Rubidoux, Cross Rock Area
Map 5

Rubidoux, Cross Rock Area
Map 5
1. **Candlestick Mantel 5.10d**
2. **Swinger 5.7**
3. **Funk U Later 5.11d**
4. **Funky Dike 5.11a**
5. **Funk U Flakes 5.9**
6. **A Minor Distraction 5.12a** TR
7. **Muzzle Loader B1**
8. **Minor Mantel 5.11** ★
9. **Ultra Sheer 5.11+**
10. **Cave Chimney 5.4**
11. **Magic Fingers Traverse 5.10**
12. **Moon Mantel 5.11+** Mantel slopers at base of flake.
13. **A Major Concept 5.12** TR or A3 lead.
14. **Friction Slab 5.7** Many variations.
15. **The Jam Crack 5.4** ★
16. **Smooth Sole Direct 5.11a** ★ TR
17. **Smooth Sole Right 5.10c** TR
18. **The T Crack 5.6**
19. **The Finger Crack 5.10a** ★ Lieback.
20. **Diagonal Crack 5.7** Hand traverse or lieback.
21. **Skidder 5.11d**
22. **In My Time of Dimes B1**
23. **Sierra Club Chimney 5.3**
24. **Mr. Nice Guy 5.11c** TR

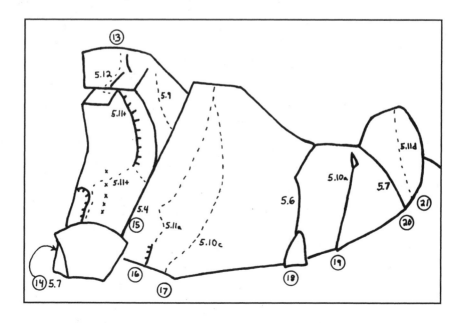

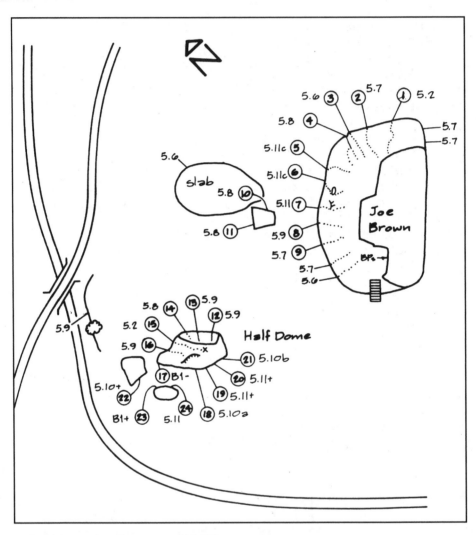

**Rubidoux, Joe Brown and Half Dome
Map 6**

Rubidoux, Joe Brown and Half Dome
Map 6
1. **Zig Zag 5.2**
2. **Direct Tissima 5.7** TR
3. **The Edge 5.6** TR
4. **Waterchute 5.8 TR ★** Direct finish is 5.9.
5. **Unisloper 5.11c TR ★**
6. **The Eye 5.11c TR ★** Reach problem.
7. **Power Pack 5.11a-5.11c TR ★** Easier for tall people.
8. **Sack Relig 5.9** TR
9. **Scoop Face 5.7 TR ★** Many variations.
10. **Double Helix 5.8**
11. **Free Feels 5.8** Scary mantel.
12. **Direct Northwast Face 5.9 ★** Left crack.
13. **Tissiack 5.9 ★** Right crack.
14. **Zenith 5.8** Face right of cracks.
15. **Cable Route 5.2 ★**
16. **Steck-Salathe 5.9**
17. **Catherine's Wheel B1-** Elimination problem.
18. **Trapeze 5.10a ★**
19. **The Transvestite 5.11** TR
20. **Harrison's Peanut 5.11+**
21. **Brainiac 5.10b**
22. **Overhung 5.10+** Yabo start.
23. **Pink Bug B1+**
24. **Black Knat 5.11**

Sequence of "In the Picture" (5.11+), Island Wall, Rubidoux.
Photos by Dean Kubani.

**Rubidoux, Borson's Wall Area
Map 7**
1. Castaways 5.12 TR* Dyno.
2. Beetle Juice 5.10c
3. Kryptonite 5.11
4. Techtite 5.10+ TR
5. Bombs Away 5.11a TR
6. Auto Pilot 5.11b TR*
7. Pilot to Bombardier 5.11+ TR
8. Tail gunner 5.11d TR
9. Ballin' the Jack 5.11
10. The Hour Glass 5.10
11. The Ex B1
12. Big Rock Boy's Mantel B1
13. Borson's Mantel 5.11a
    Mantel or dyno.
14. Borson's Lieback 5.9

15. Black Pinch 5.10c ★
16. Masterlock 5.11+ ★
17. Borson's Left Side 5.10a
18. Beryllium 5.9 TR
19. Rhodochrosite 5.10d TR
20. Cornerstone 5.8
21. Third Pitch of Astroman
    5.10c TR
22. Black Block Face 5.11b TR
23. Blockhead 5.10d TR Crack.
24. Falling Off 5.10b TR
25. Falling Away 5.10c TR
26. Falling Rocks 5.10d TR
27. Falling Asleep 5.9 TR
28. Step On It 5.10+ TR
29. Head Stone 5.8
30. Iron Cross 5.12 TR
31. Black Block Arête 5.12 TR

*Todd Battery
on the
extremely long
dyno on
"Castaway's"
(5.12),
Rubidoux.*

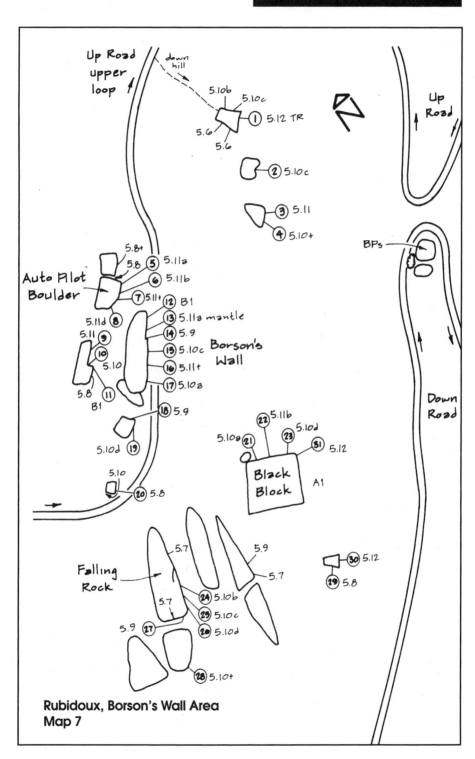

Rubidoux, Borson's Wall Area
Map 7

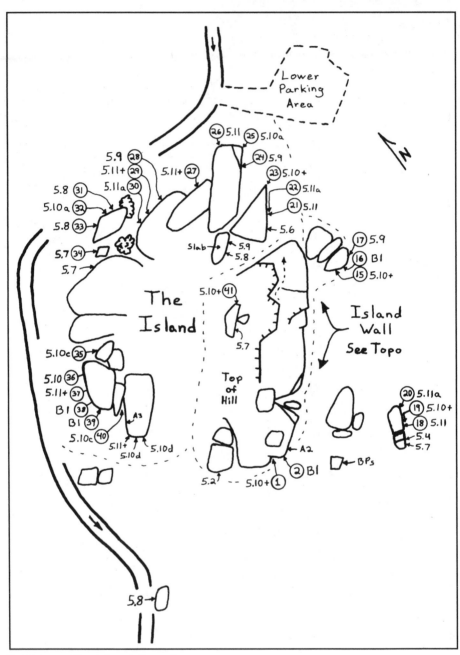

Rubidoux, The Island Overview
Map 8

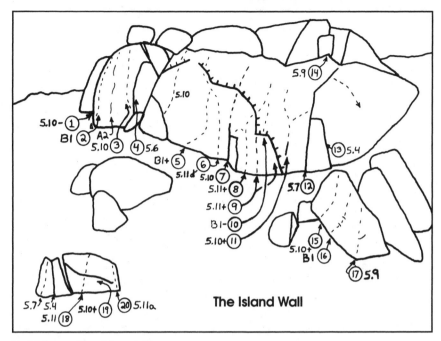

The Island Wall

Rubidoux, The Island Area
Map 8

1. **The White Book 5.10a**
2. **K.P.'s Arête B1** TR Use extra large cheatstone.
3. **Contest Special 5.10** TR
4. **Bootleg Crack 5.6** Wide.
5. **Middle of the Road Madness B1+**
6. **Silverstone 5.11d ★** TR
7. **Ashtar Roof 5.10** TR Seam to roof crux.
8. **Teflon 5.11+** Possible escape off left, after crux moves.
9. **In the Picture 5.11+ ★** Lieback. Direct start or undercling.
10. **Overexposed B1- ★**
11. **Five Niner 5.10+ ★** Direct finish 5.10+; escape right 5.10.
12. **Island Crack 5.7 ★**
13. **Flake Variation 5.4**
14. **The Entertainer 5.9** TR
15. **Spencer 5.10+**
16. **Matt B1**
17. **Dutzi 5.9**
18. **Crosswalk 5.11**
19. **One Way Street 5.10+** Traverse.
20. **Franklin Street 5.11a ★**
21. **Tiny Crack 5.11**
22. **Linear Fracture 5.11a** Traverse.
23. **Cerebral Spinal Fluid 5.10+**
24. **More Mantels 5.9**
25. **Mantel Place 5.10a**
26. **Mother's Little Helper 5.11** TR
27. **Inscription Mantel 5.11+**
28. **Peppertree Crack 5.9**
29. **Peppertree Crank 5.11+**
30. **Peppertree Problem 5.11a**
31. **Dynamite Flake 5.8**
32. **Dynamite Face 5.10a**
33. **Dynamite Crack 5.8**
34. **Tombstone 5.7** Corner is off-limits.
35. **Holes 5.10c**
36. **Brainstorm 5.10**
37. **Mantelectomy 5.11+**
38. **Presto Digitator B1**
39. **Big Eric's Dyno B1**
40. **Her Crack 5.10c** TR Bombay chimney.
41. **Hugs and Pinches 5.10+**

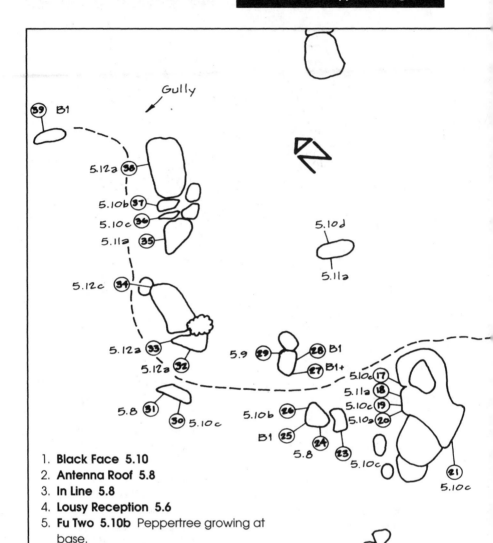

1. **Black Face 5.10**
2. **Antenna Roof 5.8**
3. **In Line 5.8**
4. **Lousy Reception 5.6**
5. **Fu Two 5.10b** Peppertree growing at base.
6. **Ten-Cent Phone Call 5.10b**
7. **Busy Signal 5.9**
8. **Plugged Nickel 5.10b**
9. **Double Eagle 5.11b** ★ TR Arête.
10. **The Talon 5.10b** Seam.
11. **Let Your Fingers Do the Walking 5.11d**
12. **Just Try Looking 5.11d** TR
13. **Blind Faith 5.10+**
14. **The Black Crack 5.11**
15. **The Squirt Gun 5.11** ★
16. **Quickdraw 5.10**
17. **A Fear of Flying 5.10c**
18. **Bugger Any Which Way You Can 5.11a**

19. **Bugger As Fast As You Can 5.10c**
20. **Bugger As Bugger Can Be 5.10a**
21. **The Musket 5.10c**
22. **The Potato Bug 5.11c**
23. **Six Gun 5.10c**
24. **Spurless 5.8**
25. **The Bull's Eye B1** Seam.
26. **The Noose 5.10b**
27. **5.10b on the Outside B1+**
28. **Hair Trigger B1** ★
29. **Bugle Call 5.9**

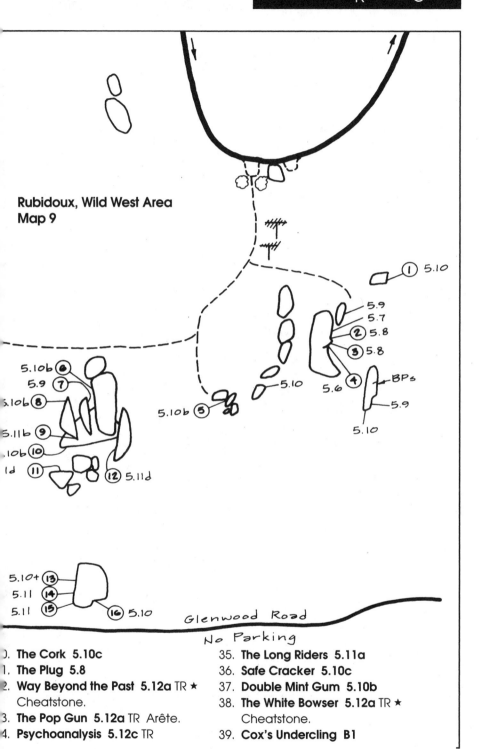

Rubidoux, Wild West Area
Map 9

1 5.10
5.9
5.7
2 5.8
3 5.8
5.10b 6
5.9 7
5.10
5.10b 8
5.10b 5
5.6 4 BPs
5.11b 9
5.9
5.10b 10
5.10
1d 11
12 5.11d

5.10+ 13
5.11 14
5.11 15
16 5.10   Glenwood Road
No Parking

). The Cork 5.10c
1. The Plug 5.8
2. Way Beyond the Past 5.12a TR ★
   Cheatstone.
3. The Pop Gun 5.12a TR Arête.
4. Psychoanalysis 5.12c TR

35. The Long Riders 5.11a
36. Safe Cracker 5.10c
37. Double Mint Gum 5.10b
38. The White Bowser 5.12a TR ★
    Cheatstone.
39. Cox's Undercling B1

Central Riverside Area Map

The Central Riverside area map below shows street access to the following areas: **Menifee, Juniper Flats, Bernasconi Ridge**, the **Hemet areas**, and the **Glue-on area**.

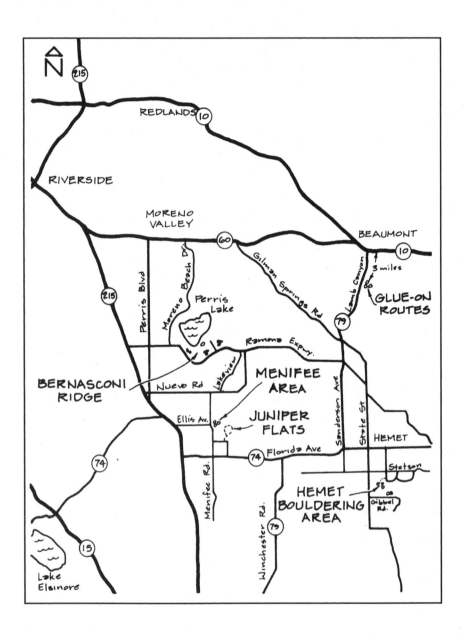

BERNASCONI RIDGE

Everyone who's ever driven the Ramona Expressway has probably thought that there must be climbing all over this hill, and indeed there is. **Bernasconi Wall** is a small bluff with quality rock that offers top-roping and bouldering. The **Mushroom Boulders** sport a couple of classic problems. Slab routes and bouldering are also found just north of Bernasconi Beach Road. With a little exploration on this legally accessible hill, many quality climbs will someday be found.

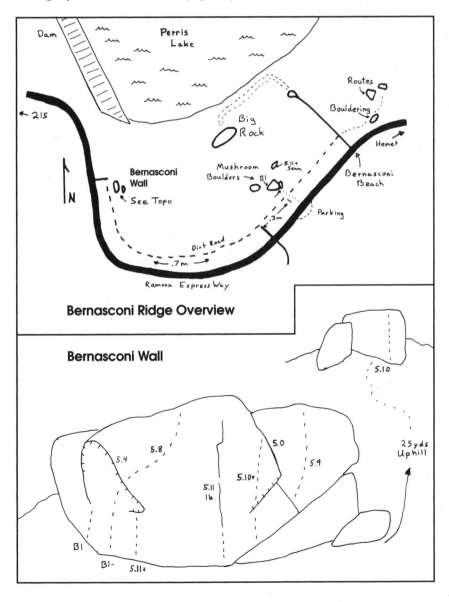

Bernasconi Ridge Overview

Bernasconi Wall

NUEVO AREAS

The two very fine areas of **Juniper Flats** and **Menifee** could be considered the Mount Woodson of Riverside County. Huge granite boulders litter the hillsides and seem to go on forever. Unfortunately, the boulders are so big that few real boulder problems exist—mostly top-rope routes. The access is great: no manzanita thrash to negotiate—just knee high fox tails. The large, egg-shaped boulders are often split by perfect cracks or cracked wide open, revealing beautifully textured rock. The areas described in this guide have legal access at this time and seem to have no nearby housing developments pending.

Nuevo Areas Overview

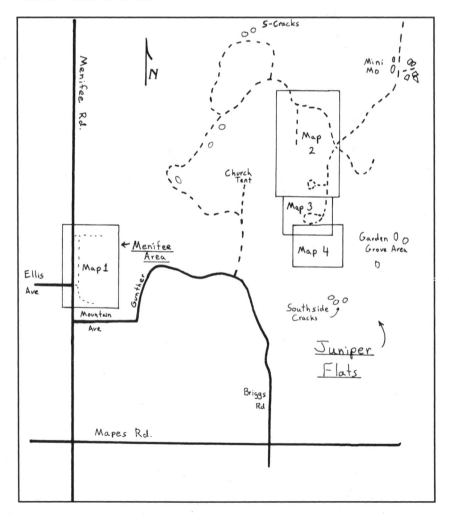

Sam Owing was the first to explore this area, and soon after, Kerwin Klein, Curtis Shannon, Craig Britton, and Jean Bonner developed the Menifee and Juniper Flats areas.

The area is somewhat tainted by local abuses, namely motorcycles, graffiti, and dumped trash. Poison oak will be found on the north slopes. Rattlers and other snakes are common. Climbing is good fall through spring. Summer evenings are also good.

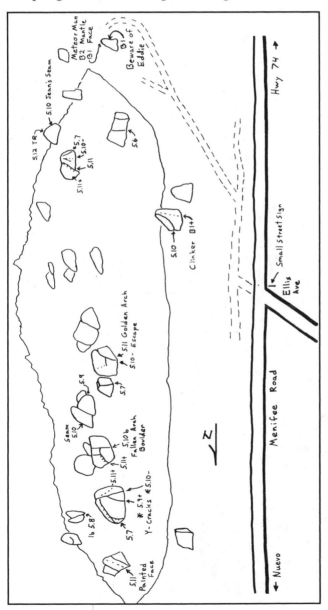

Menifee Area
Topo 1

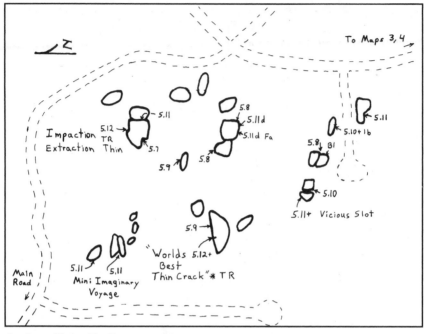

Juniper Flats, North
Map 2

Bob Van Bell on "The Lizard King Dihedral" (5.10 c), Juniper Flats. Photo by Kerwin Klein.

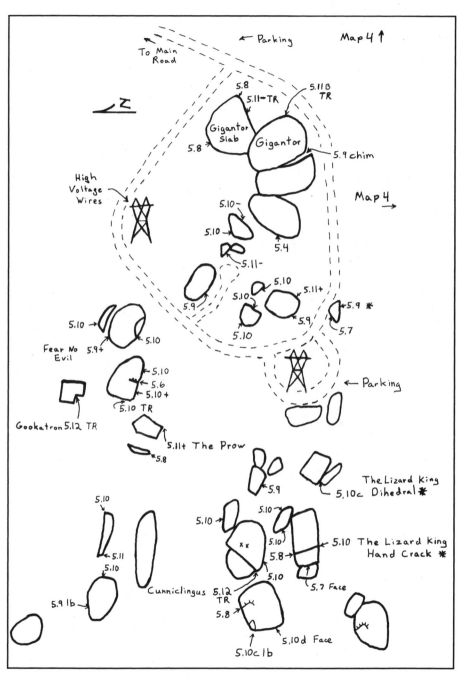

Juniper Flats Center
Map 3

Juniper Flats, South
Map 4

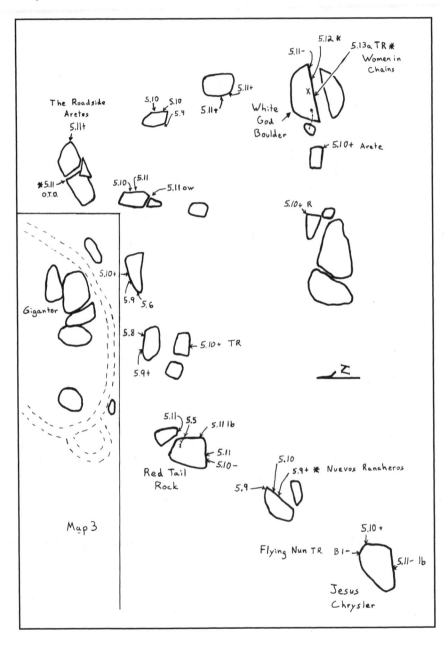

The Roadside Aretes
5.11+

**5.11 O.T.O.

5.10   5.11
5.11 ow

5.10 5.10
5.9

5.11+

5.11+

White God Boulder

5.12 *
5.11−
5.13a TR *
Women in Chains
X

5.10+ Arete

5.10+ R

Gigantor

5.10+

5.9 5.6

5.8
5.9+

5.10+ TR

N

5.11 5.5
5.11 lb

5.11
5.10−

Red Tail Rock

5.9

5.10
5.9+ * Nuevos Rancheros

Map 3

Flying Nun TR B1−

5.10+
5.11− lb

Jesus Chrysler

HIGHWAY 79 GLUE-ON ROUTES

On Highway 79, just south of Highway 10 in Beaumont, is a large over-hanging boulder with several top-ropes on glued-on holds. **See map on page 172.**

HEMET BOULDERING

Bouldering and top-roping are found just outside of Hemet on Gibbel Road and off of Grand Avenue. **See the map below for locations.**

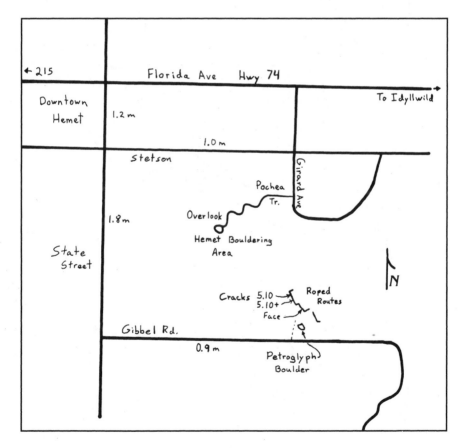

Hemet Bouldering Road Access Map

IDYLLWILD

Three bouldering areas are found near **Idyllwild:**
Humber Park. County Park, and **South Ridge.** Climbing
is practical in Idyllwild May through October.

Idyllwild Areas Overview

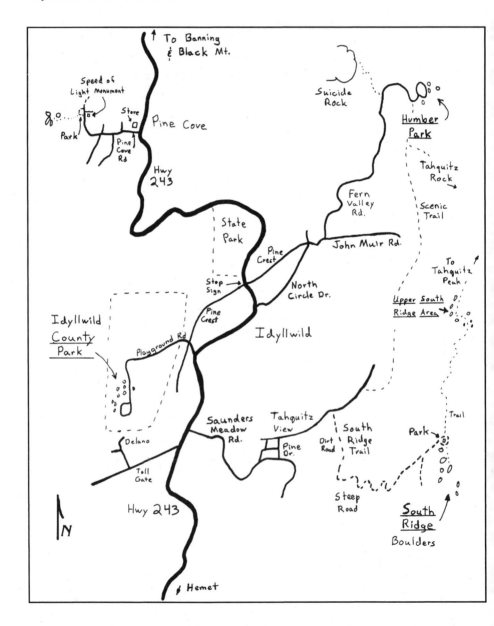

IDYLLWILD- RELATIVITY BOULDERS

No climbing allowed.

The **Relativity Boulders** in Pine Cove are located near the site of the 1926 speed-of-light experiments led by Nobel laureate Dr. Albert A. Michelson. These boulders are on private property and neither climbing nor trespassing is allowed. The map below is reproduced here for historical purposes only.

Idyllwild, Relativity Boulders

IDYLLWILD- HUMBER PARK

Humber Park has some good bouldering in the parking area. At the top of the loop is the **Nose Boulder** and a short face with problems next to the road. Below the loop is a boulder with a few problems, including **Weasels Ripped My Flesh** (B1+) on the steep section section next to a tree. More boulders are found above the road, the best being the **Spiral Tree Boulder**, about 100 yards above and to the right of the Nose Boulder.

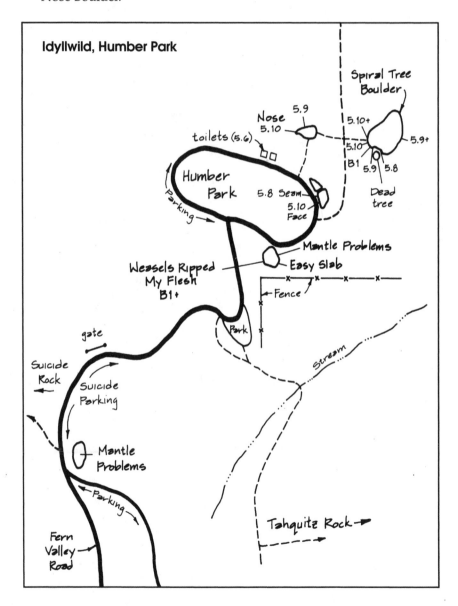

IDYLLWILD- SOUTH RIDGE BOULDERING

These spectacular boulders, high on the ridge south of Tahquitz offer the best bouldering in the Idyllwild area. The area consists of many huge granite boulders with problems of 10 to 30 feet in length, characterized by face climbing similar to Suicide Rock. A steep dirt road provides access right up to the first boulder. The road is pot-holed and vehicles with low clearance will probably have trouble getting past some sections. Several intermediate parking locations are available.

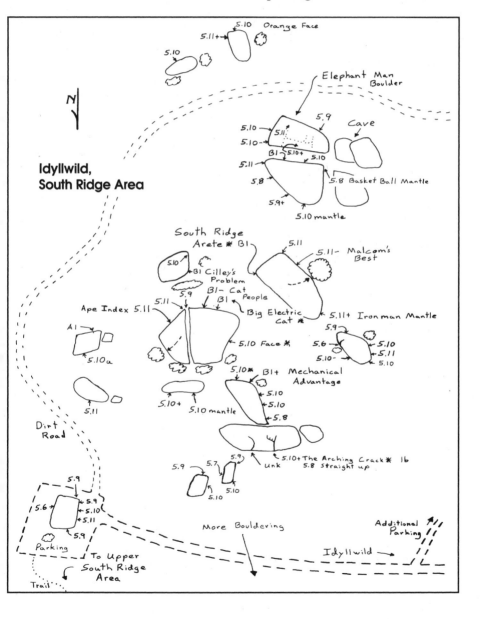

The classic **South Ridge Arête** (B1/B1+) is the most noteworthy problem on the ridge. Twenty feet of overhanging knob pinching and arête climbing have turned back many efforts by strong boulderers. Skip Guerin was the first to claim this prize. Mike Paul's **Mechanical Advantage** (B1+) and **Big Electric Cat** (B1) are some other quality hard problems. Most problems are 5.10 or harder and there is little available for the beginner at this granite playground.

A 30 minute hike up the South Ridge Trail brings you to the **Upper South Ridge** area. Many boulders along the way have good problems. Once you get to the obvious cave view, the concentrated—but limited—bouldering begins. A good place to relax and put the boots on is at the **Yabo** area.

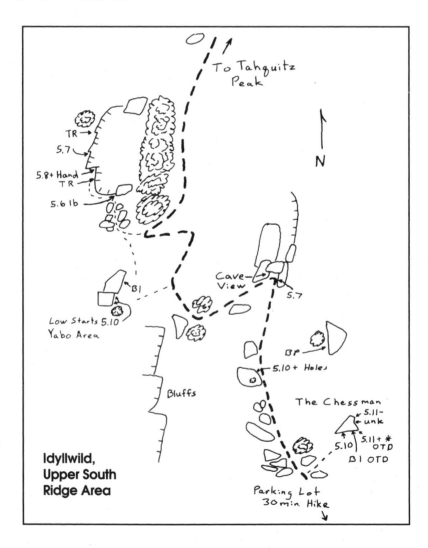

Idyllwild,
Upper South
Ridge Area

IDYLLWILD- COUNTY PARK

Idyllwild County Park has a considerable number of climbable granite boulders. The park is better known as an area for locals rather than a destination area since the **South Ridge** or **Black Mountain** are much better alternatives. The boulders are found on the west side of the campground lurking amongst the trees and brush. Since many of the boulders are quite small, mantles are numerous. **The Granite Wave, AH Boulder**, and **Mushroom Boulder** are good-sized rocks and offer excellent face and crack problems. A $3.00 fee must be paid at the entrance gate to park inside the park, although you can park on Delano Road and walk in for free.

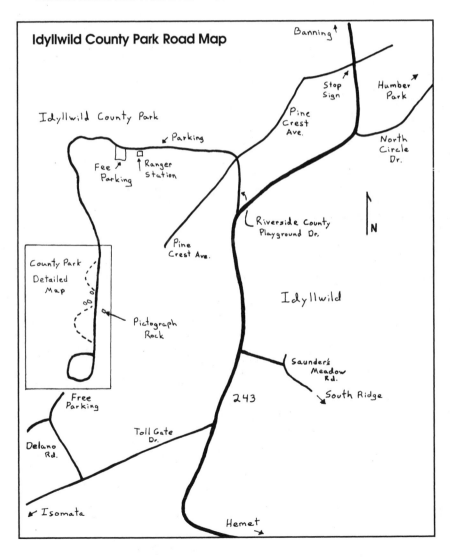

Idyllwild County Park Road Map

Idyllwild County Park Overview

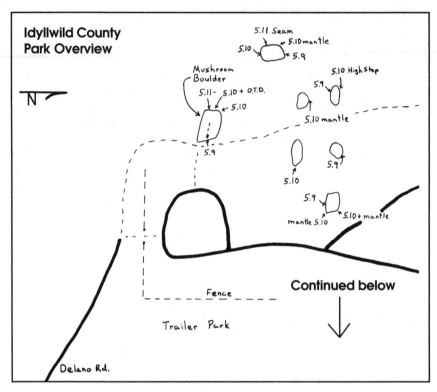

N

Idyllwild County Park Overview

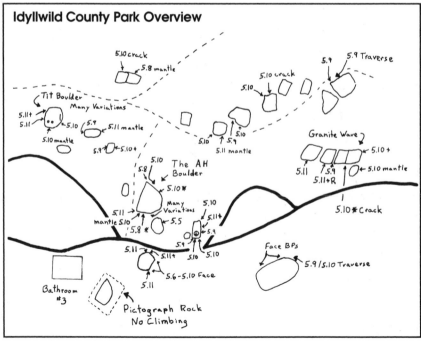

BLACK MOUNTAIN

Black Mountain is another of the many great granite bouldering areas in Southern California. The mountain's extensive boulderfields stretch beyond the furthest reaches of view, and there will be exploration of new boulders for years to come. The high altitude setting with open

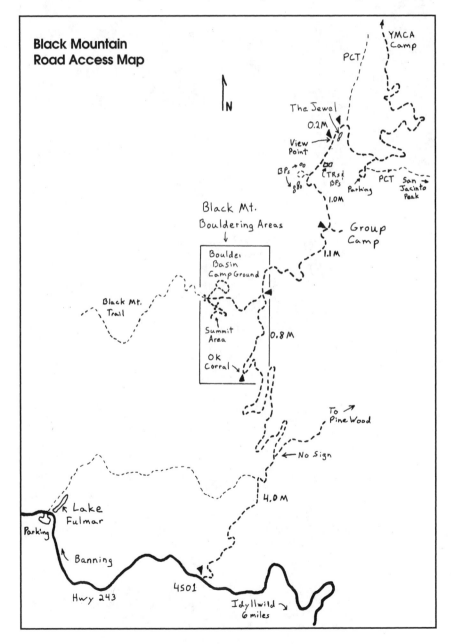

**Black Mountain
Road Access Map**

↑N

YMCA Camp

PCT

The Jewel

0.2M

View Point

BPs ⁰⁰
8o
ETRs &
BPs

Parking

1.0M

PCT

San Jacinto Peak

Black Mt.
Bouldering Areas
↓

Boulder Basin Camp Ground

Black Mt. Trail

Summit Area

Ok Corral

Group Camp

1.1M

0.8M

To Pine Wood

←No Sign

4.0M

Lake Fulmar

Parking

Banning

Hwy 243

4S01

Idyllwild ↘
6 miles

Craig Fry on the "Visor Lip" (5.11+), Black Mountain Summit Area.

Kevin Daniels on "Way Too High" (5.11+ R), Boulder Basin. Photo by Bill Freeman.

pine forest provides easy access and sometimes soft landings for the large boulders. The original Black Mountain areas developed (**Boulder Basin Campground** and **OK Corral**) were characterized by small holds and big fall potential. The newer areas (**Summit** and **North Ridge**) offer good alternatives to the OTD/R classics. The boulders are smaller, knobby, overhanging, and have good landings. Many of these newer problems are short, with sit-down starts.

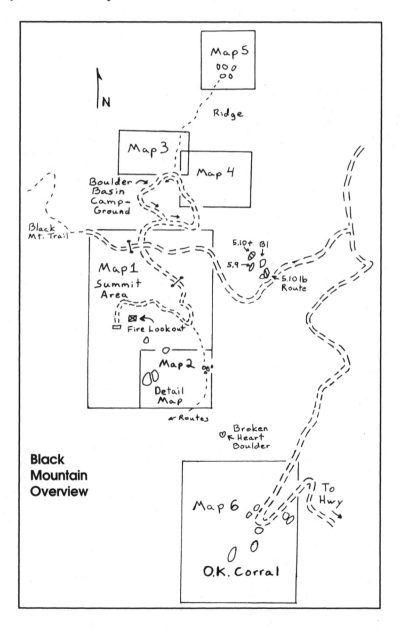

Black Mountain Overview

Black Mountain has become quite popular over the years since it was first developed in the mid-seventies. Once again, John Long was the first to maximize the potential of the area, and he established many hard classics with his typical flair of fright factor added to each. **Where Boneheads Dare** (B1) ★, **Moroccan Roll** (B1-), and **The Largo Stem** (B1-) are some examples.

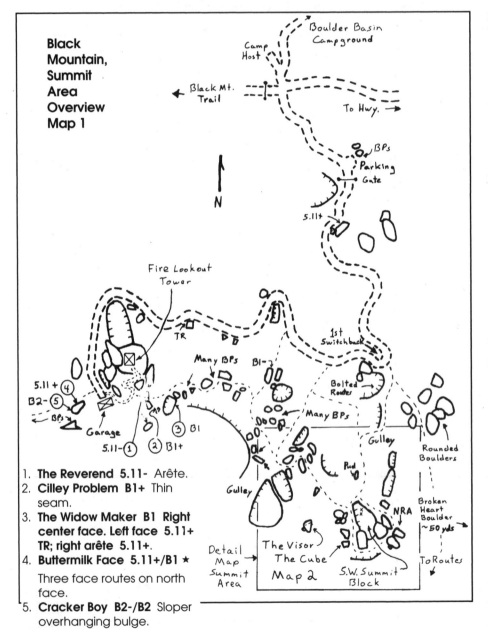

1. **The Reverend 5.11-** Arête.
2. **Cilley Problem B1+** Thin seam.
3. **The Widow Maker B1 Right** center face. Left face 5.11+ TR; right arête 5.11+.
4. **Buttermilk Face 5.11+/B1** ★

    Three face routes on north face.

5. **Cracker Boy B2-/B2** Sloper overhanging bulge.

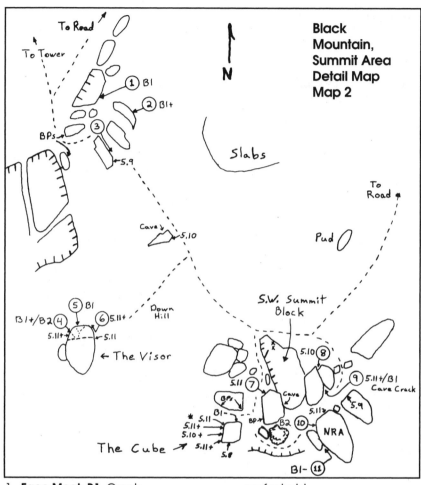

1. **Face Meat B1** Crank.
2. **Face Meat Mantel B1+**
3. **Fingerboard Traverse 5.9/5.11+**
4. **Can Opener B1+/B2** Variations.
5. **Center Visor B1/B2-** ★ Many variations.
6. **Visor Lip 5.11+** ★ Mantel over lip is crux.
7. **Yosemite Problem 5.11** Loose wafer hold.
8. **Easy Mumblage 5.10** Cave start.
9. **Mumbles Roof 5.11+/B1-** ★ Cave hand crank.
10. **NRA B2** ★ Scoops, sit-down start.
11. **Lower NRA B1-** ★ Low start, many variations.

There are three main areas at Black Mountain: **The OK Corral, Boulder Basin Campground**, and the **Summit Area**. The Summit area also has many short routes including the **Rainbow Arête**, a five star 5.12a route. Quality bouldering can also be found two miles further up the road just past the group campground. The YMCA Camp, six miles up the road past the "Boulder Basin" intersection, has additional huge boulders with some routes established.

Do not park in the Boulder Basin campground unless you want to pay the camping fee. Park just outside and walk in (do not block the gate). Black Mountain Road (4S01) is closed during the winter until late May.

Season: The elevation is over 7,000 feet at Black Mountain and summer is the best time for bouldering.

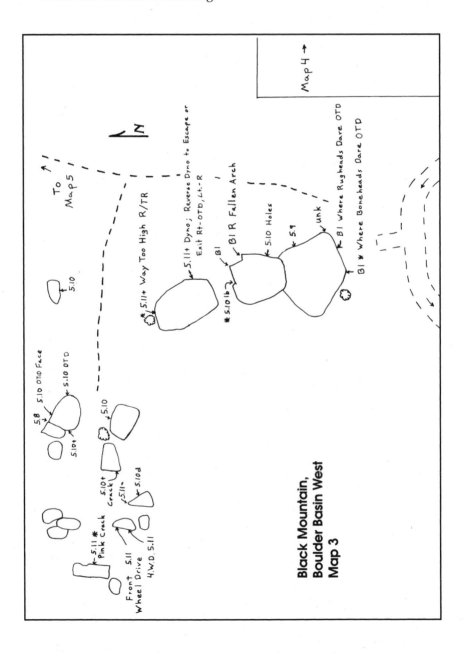

Black Mountain,
Boulder Basin West
Map 3

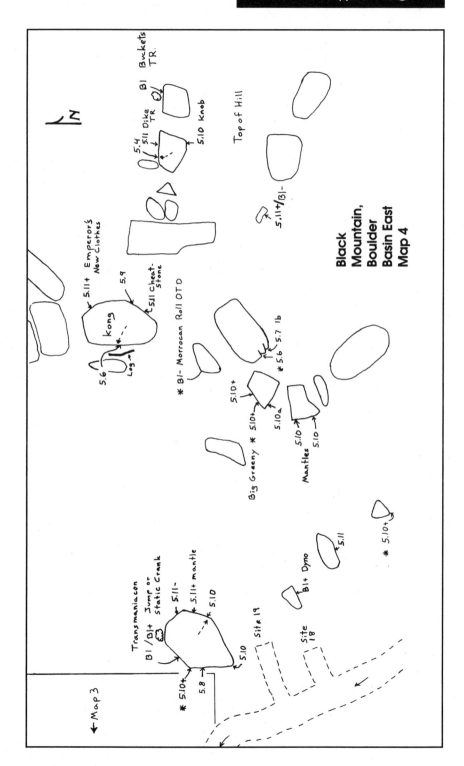

Black
Mountain,
Boulder
Basin East
Map 4

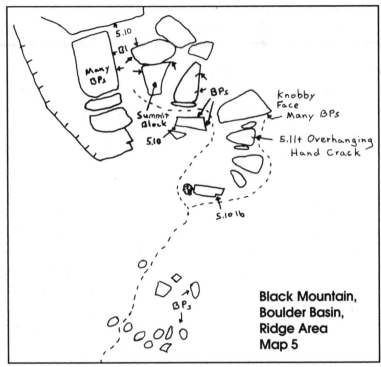

**Black Mountain,
Boulder Basin,
Ridge Area
Map 5**

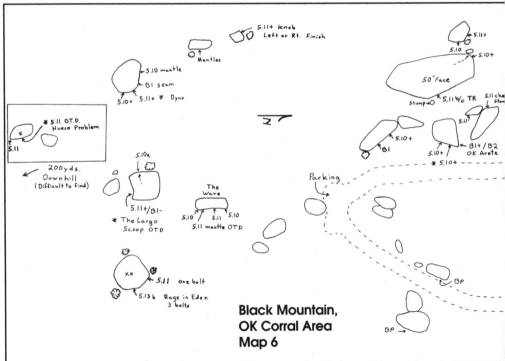

**Black Mountain,
OK Corral Area
Map 6**

by Ron Amick

San Diego is ear-to-ear boulders and then some. Virtually out of control in terms of volume and density, they gather unchecked throughout the county, forming ominous gangs which loiter amongst remote hillsides and valleys with impunity.

Once thought to be without climbing value, these boulder packs have long stood in smug isolation, their privacy protected by this misconception as well as the hundreds of yards of dense chaparral which invariably must be negotiated before any type of evaluation as to quality and potential can be ventured. No amount of inspection from afar—be it with good binoculars or long range photospectrometry—can determine whether a given mob is priceless or worthless. No, one must undertake to strike out through inestimable vegetation and actually feel the holds in person before they will divulge their secrets.

The three hour hell-hike to a grunt-hunk which looks like El Cap from the road is a legacy in these parts. Likewise, many a classic problem has been gleaned from some squat and homely buttknuckle next to the road, once someone takes the time to look at its backside. The point is that nothing can be written off without inspection, and this realization has spurred exploratory probes into rocks which had been dismissed as bogus, mostly with positive results.

A by-product of this new determination to find out what's really out there is a willingness to plunge and grumble through brush-barriers once considered impenetrable by any means save parachute or hovercraft. While it certainly is possible to thrash oneself into situations in the deep brush which would make hell seem like Club Med, this happens far less often than one would expect. The best advice a guide can offer regarding the vast unknown boulderfields is to find 'em, get to 'em, jump on 'em, and please don't pound on 'em.

This section will only focus on the most popular established bouldering areas around San Diego, giving what info is practical. Plenty has been left unaccounted for, so don't assume this to be a complete reference. Talk to local climbers to find the new or obscure areas if that's your bag.

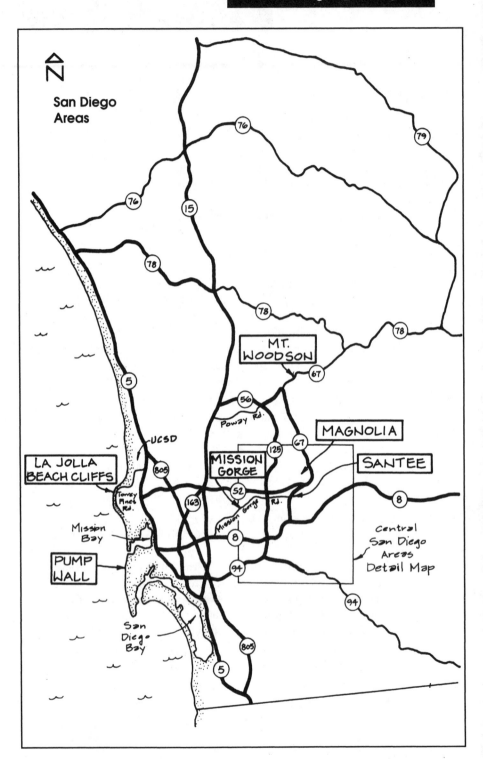

Greg Epperson demonstrates the proper technique for slippery mantles on the "Pink Boulder," Mission Gorge area. Photo by Ron Amick.

*Below:
Ron Amick on "The Light Bulb" (5.9) at Santee. Photo by Greg Epperson.*

MOUNT WOODSON

This remarkable area has every type of climbing, including some classic crack lines, which were Woodson's original claim to fame. While the cracks are deluxe, Woodson is far more than a crack climbing area in that face routes outnumber cracks by at least five to one; and those face routes are every bit as good as the best crack lines.

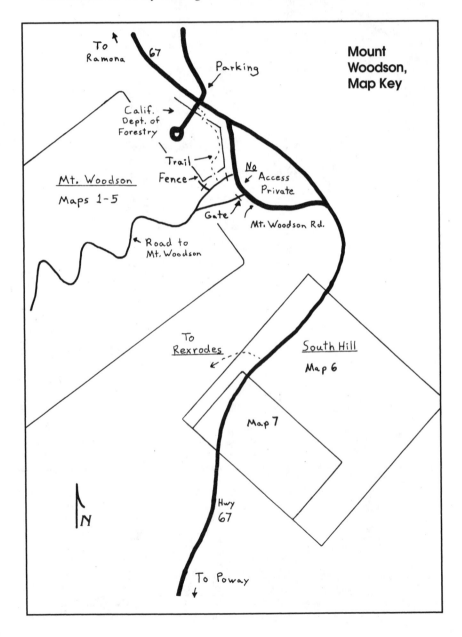

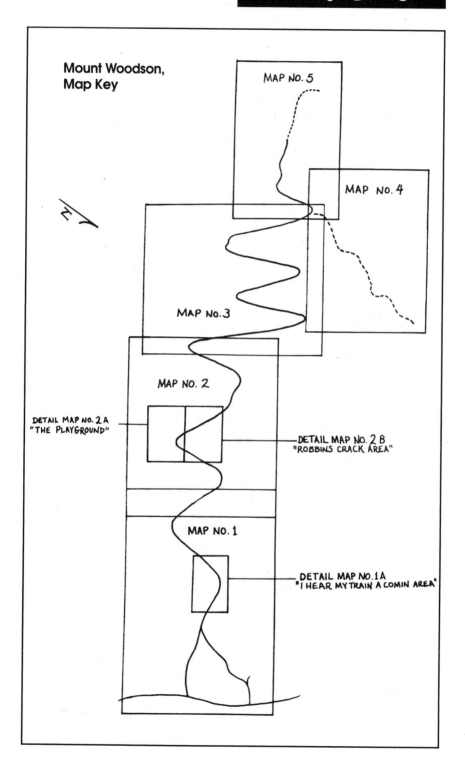

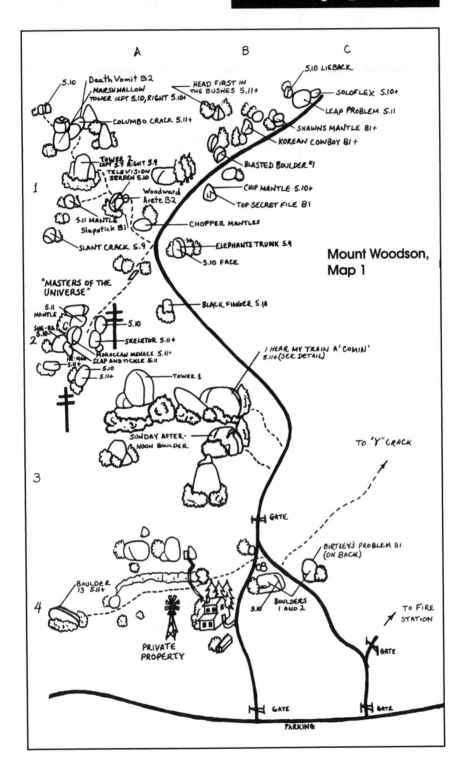

A   B   C

5.10 LIEBACK

5.10   Death Vomit B2

MARSHMALLOW
TOWER LEFT 5.10, RIGHT 5.10+

HEAD FIRST IN
THE BUSHES 5.11+

SOLOFLEX 5.10+

LEAP PROBLEM 5.11

COLUMBO CRACK 5.11+

SHAWNS MANTLE B1+

KOREAN COWBOY B1+

TOWER 2
LEFT 5.7 RIGHT 5.9
TELEVISION
SCREEN 5.10

BLASTED BOULDER #1

Woodward
Arete B2

CHIP MANTLE 5.10+

TOP SECRET FILE B1

1

5.11 MANTLE
Slapstick B1

CHOPPER MANTLES

SLANT CRACK 5.9

ELEPHANTS TRUNK 5.9

5.10 FACE

**Mount Woodson,
Map 1**

"MASTERS OF THE
UNIVERSE"

BLACK FINGER 5.10

5.11
MANTLE

SHE-RA
5.10

5.10

2

SKELETOR 5.11+

HE-MAN
5.11+

MOROCCAN MENACE 5.11+
SLAP AND TICKLE 5.11

5.10

5.11+

TOWER 1

I HEAR MY TRAIN A' COMIN'
5.11+ (SEE DETAIL)

SUNDAY AFTER-
NOON BOULDER

TO "Y" CRACK

3

GATE

BIRTLEY'S PROBLEM B1
(ON BACK)

BOULDER
13 5.11+

BOULDERS
1 AND 2

5.10

TO FIRE
STATION

4

PRIVATE
PROPERTY

GATE

GATE   GATE

PARKING

Woodson was "discovered" around the mid- to late 1960s, when locals succeeded in dragging some of Yosemite's finest hardmen down to check out the allegedly classic crack lines there. These valley boys were probably the finest climbers in the world at the time, and they picked some of Woodson's finest plums, establishing some climbs which were as hard as anything else in America.

Royal Robbins was the first to pay a visit, and he was shown a beautiful 25-foot crack which locals told him they had done. What they neglected to add was that they had aided the thing. Not to be out-climbed, Robbins cranked it in a superb effort, unwittingly doing the first free ascent of **Robbins Crack** (5.10a) at a time when 5.10 was as extreme as it got. Awed by Robbins' achievement, nobody ever let on that they hadn't even tried a free ascent of the route, and Robbins went back to the Valley with tales of Woodson's exceptional hardmen and great cracks. Thus was born Woodson's reputation as a land of hard cracks and hard crack climbers.

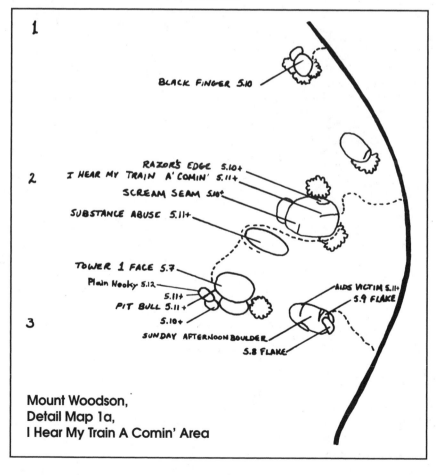

Mount Woodson,
Detail Map 1a,
I Hear My Train A Comin' Area

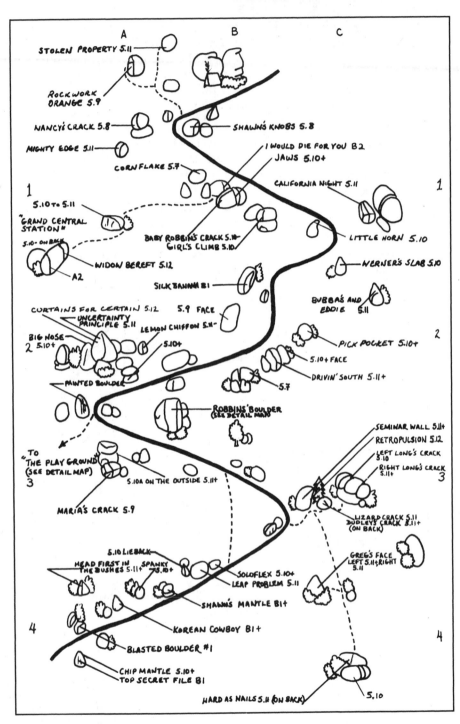

STOLEN PROPERTY 5.11

ROCKWORK ORANGE 5.9

NANCY'S CRACK 5.8

MIGHTY EDGE 5.11

CORN FLAKE 5.7

SHAWN'S KNOBS 5.8

I WOULD DIE FOR YOU B2
JAWS 5.10+

CALIFORNIA NIGHT 5.11

1

5.10 TO 5.11
"GRAND CENTRAL STATION"

5.10- ON BACK

WIDOW BEREFT 5.12

A2

BABY ROBBINS CRACK 5.10
GIRL'S CLIMB 5.10

SILK BANANA B1

LITTLE HORN 5.10

WERNER'S SLAB 5.10

1

CURTAINS FOR CERTAIN 5.12
UNCERTAINTY PRINCIPLE 5.11
BIG NOSE 5.10+
2

PAINTED BOULDER

5.9 FACE

LEMON CHIFFON 5.11

5.10+

BUBBA'S AND EDDIE 5.11

PICK POCKET 5.10+

5.10+ FACE

DRIVIN' SOUTH 5.11+

5.7

2

ROBBINS BOULDER
(SEE DETAIL MAP)

TO
"THE PLAY GROUND"
(SEE DETAIL MAP)
3

5.10A ON THE OUTSIDE 5.11+

MARIA'S CRACK 5.9

SEMINAR WALL 5.11+
RETROPULSION 5.12
LEFT LONG'S CRACK 5.10
RIGHT LONG'S CRACK 5.11+

3

LIZARD CRACK 5.11
DUDLEY'S CRACK 5.11+
(ON BACK)

5.10 LIEBACK
HEAD FIRST IN THE BUSHES 5.11+
SPANKY 5.10+

SOLOFLEX 5.10+
LEAP PROBLEM 5.11

SHAWN'S MANTLE B1+

KOREAN COWBOY B1+

BLASTED BOULDER #1

CHIP MANTLE 5.10+
TOP SECRET FILE B1

GREG'S FACE
LEFT 5.11; RIGHT 5.11

4

4

HARD AS NAILS 5.11 (ON BACK)

5.10

Mount Woodson, Map 2

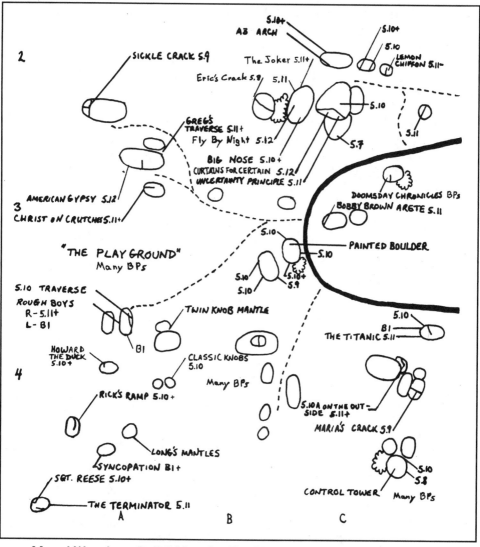

Mount Woodson, Detail Map 2a, The Playground Area

A few years later, in the early 1970s, the next generation of valley hot-shots made the pilgrimage to the mysterious Mt. Woodson and its legendary cracks. Several trips south by the likes of Bachar, Long, Kauk and others resulted in more classic routes of state-of-the-art technical difficulty. Fruits of that era included **Hear My Train A-Comin'** (5.11c), **Driving South** (5.11d), **California Night** (5.11b), and more. Woodson's reputation as a crack climbing Mecca was now written in stone—a misleading perception which persists to this day.

By the early seventies the locals had caught up to the standards of the day and were busy establishing hundreds of classic routes. Known as the Poway Mountain Boys, Rick Piggott and Greg Cameron were the most active climbers at this time. In 1971, Werner Landry started his annual (more or less) Great Western Bouldering Championship, which rotated among San Diego bouldering areas. This event brought in a considerable amount of competition, along with many new climbers, which in turn raised the standards and led to tremendous route development. In the late seventies and eighties, Mike Paul, Allen Nelson, Bill Ramsey, Greg Epperson, Ray Olsen, Rick Piggott, Shawn Curtis and many others were responsible for the

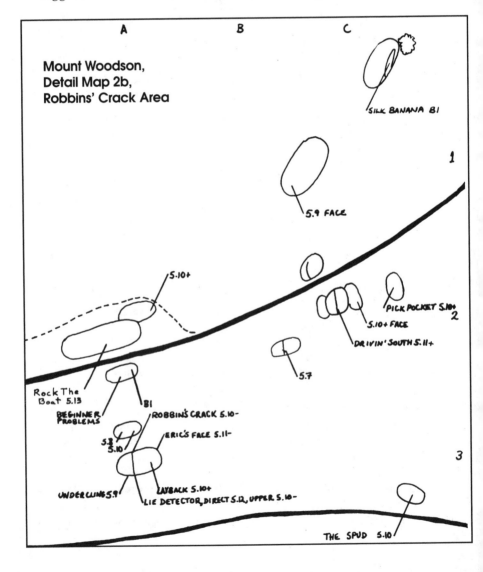

Mount Woodson,
Detail Map 2b,
Robbins' Crack Area

SILK BANANA B1

5.9 FACE

5.10+

PICK POCKET S.10+

S.10+ FACE

DRIVIN' SOUTH S. 11+

5.7

Rock The
Boat 5.13

B1

BEGINNER
PROBLEMS

ROBBINS CRACK 5.10-

ERIC'S FACE 5.11-

5.1
5.10

UNDERCLING 5.9

LAYBACK 5.10+

LIE DETECTOR DIRECT S.12, UPPER S.10-

THE SPUD 5.10

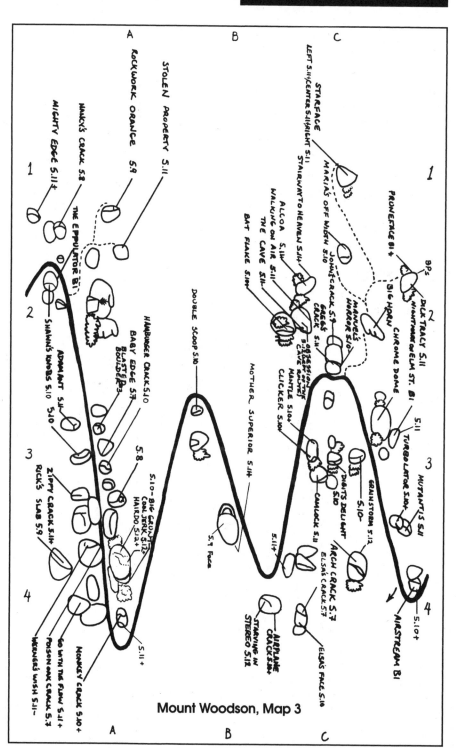

Mount Woodson, Map 3

intense development that has redefined Woodson as an area of hard mantels and faces as well as the hardest thin cracks and offwidths in San Diego County.

The rock is a granite-diorite of light color and firm composition, manifested as thousands of boulders ranging up to 120 feet in height. The average route is more like 15-30 feet, however. Potential for new routes is vast, and development has just recently begun in earnest away from the road, with plums-a-plenty being dug out of the void.

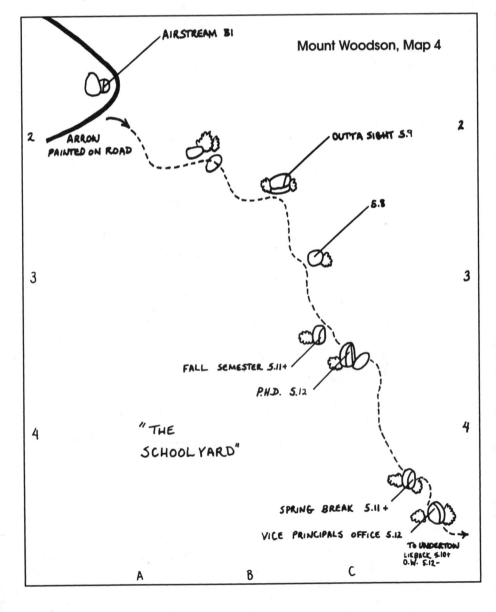

AIRSTREAM 31

Mount Woodson, Map 4

2

ARROW PAINTED ON ROAD

OUTTA SIGHT 5.9

2

5.8

3

3

FALL SEMESTER 5.11+

P.H.D. 5.12

"THE SCHOOL YARD"

4

4

SPRING BREAK 5.11+

VICE PRINCIPALS OFFICE 5.12

TO UNDERTOW
LIEBACK 5.10+
O.W. 5.12-

A   B   C

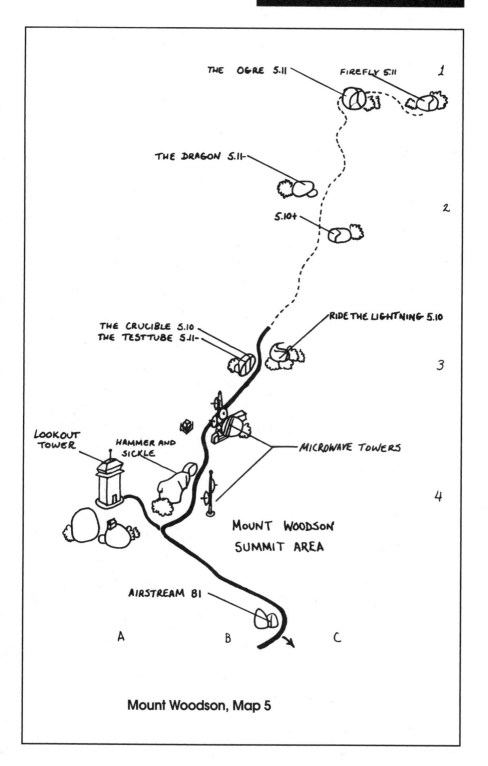

Mount Woodson, Map 5

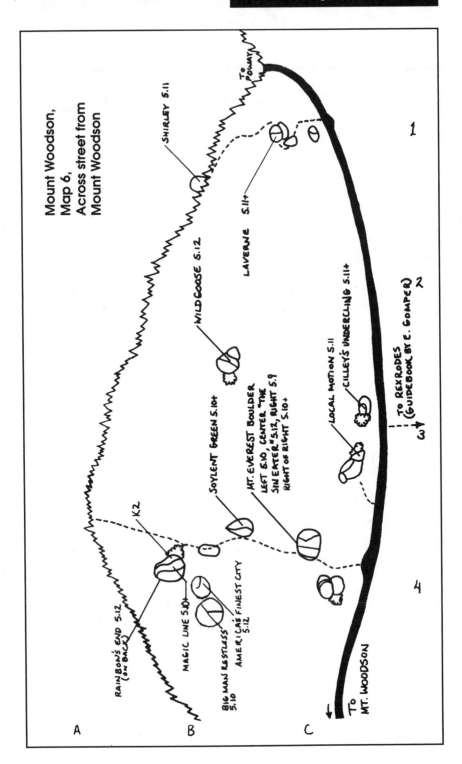

Mount Woodson,
Map 6,
Across street from
Mount Woodson

SHIRLEY 5.11

TO
POWAY

1

LAVERNE 5.11+

WILDGOOSE 5.12

2

TO REXRODES
(GUIDEBOOK BY E. GOMPER)

CILLEY'S UNDERCLING 5.11+

LOCAL MOTION 5.11

3

SOYLENT GREEN 5.10+

MT. EVEREST BOULDER
LEFT 5.10, CENTER "THE
SIN EATER" 5.12, RIGHT 5.9
RIGHT OF RIGHT 5.10+

K2

4

MAGIC LINE 5.10+

AMERICA'S FINEST CITY
5.12

RAINBOW'S END 5.12
(ON BACK)

BIG MAN RESTLESS
5.10

TO
MT. WOODSON

A

B

C

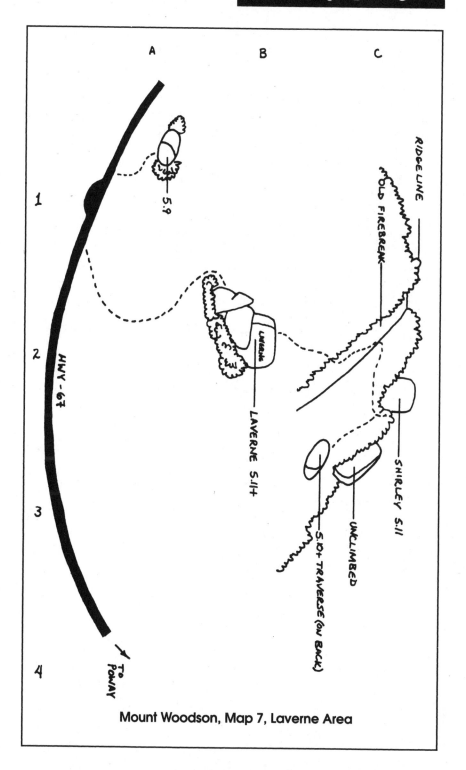

RIDGELINE

OLD FIREBREAK

5.9

HNY - 67

LAVERNE

5.11

LAVERNE 5.11+

SHIRLEY 5.11

UNCLIMBED

5.10+ TRAVERSE (ON BACK)

TO POWAY

Mount Woodson, Map 7, Laverne Area

The terrain tends to be treacherous, riven with rises and depressions, drainages and decomposed slides—all masked by a veneer of scrub which is also capable of administering punishment to unwary hikers. Landings can be bad, and should be inspected before getting off the deck. Top-rope protection may be called for on even the shortest problems for this reason, and a 30- to 50-foot runner comes in very handy for belaying anchorless boulders over the top. A 100-foot rope and Friends sized #½ to #3 are the only other equipment needed for 99% of Woodson's routes. Rap bolts tend to be in place where needed, and lead bolts are scarce (due to the short nature of the boulders.)

Climbing is possible year-round at Woodson provided one targets appropriately situated routes for the given weather. Risks include snakes, skeeters, and poor footing. The summit is around 3,300 feet, and an asphalt road goes up the east side to the top (but not for vehicles). Avoid private property along the Mt. Woodson road and at the bottom of the hill. Also beware of speeding service vehicles on the narrow road.

The previous Mount Woodson information was written by Ron Amick; the following Woodson maps were drawn by Mike Paul in 1987 and updated for this book.

Index to Mount Woodson Climbs

Name and Rating	Type	Map #	Coordinates
Adam Ant, 5.11	traverse	3	A-3
Aids Victim 5.12-	thin crack	1A	B-3
Airplane Crack, 5.10+	thin crack	3	B-4
Air Stream, 5.12	thin crack	4	A-1
Alcoa, 5.11+	lieback	3	C-2
American Gypsy, 5.12+	lieback	2A	A-3
America's Finest City, 5.12	undercling	6	B-4
Arch Crack, 5.7	chimney	3	C-4
Baby Edge, 5.7	lieback	3	A-3
Baby Robbins, 5.9+	hand crack	2	B-1
Bat Flake, 5.10+	lieback	3	B-2
Big Grunt, 5.10-	chimney	3	A-4
Big Horn, 5.8-5.10+	face	3	C-2
Big Man Restless, 5.10	offwidth	6	B-4
Big Nose, 5.10+	face	2A	B-2
Birty's Problem, B1		1	C-4
Black Finger 5.10	thin crack	1A	B-1
Bobby Brown Arête, 5.11	face	2A	C-3

Boulder 13, 5.11+	offwidth	1	A-4
Bubba's and Eddie, 5.11	face	2	C-2
California Night, 5.11	thin crack	2	C-1
Camlock, 5.11	thin crack	3	C-3
Cave, The, 5.11-	thin crack	3	B-2
Chip Mantle, 5.10+	mantel	1	B-1
Chopper Mantles, 5.10-5.11	mantel	1	A-1
Christ on Crutches, 5.11	lieback	2A	A-3
Cilley's Undercling, 5.11+	undercling	6	C-3
Classic Knobs, 5.10	face	2A	B-4
Clicker, 5.10+	undercling	3	C-3
Clicker Mantle, 5.10+	mantel	1	C-3
Columbo Crack, 5.11+	thin crack	1	A-1
Control Tower Left, 5.8	face	2A	C-4
Control Tower Right, 5.10	face	2A	C-4
Cool Jerk, 5.12+	face	3	A-4
Corn Flake, 5.7	lieback	2	B-1
Crucible, 5.10	offwidth	5	B-3
Curtains for Certain, 5.12	face	2	A-2
Death Vomit B2	mantel	1	A-1
Digit's Delight, 5.10+	thin crack	3	C-3
Doomsday Chronicles, 5.11	face	2A	C-3
Double Scoop, 5.10	mantel	3	B-3
Dragon, 5.11-	lieback	5	B-2
Drivin' South, 5.11+	thin crack	2B	C-2
Dudley Chelton's Thin Crack, 5.11+	thin crack	2	C-3
Elephant's Trunk, 5.9	hand crack	1	B-1
Elephant's Face, 5.10	face	1	B-1
Elsa's Crack, 5.6	hand	3	A-4
Eppulator, B1	face	3	A-2
Eric's Face, 5.11-	face	2B	A-3
Eric's Offwidth, 5.8	offwidth	2A	B-2
Fall Semester, 5.11+	lieback	4	B-3
Firefly, 5.11+	thin	5	C-1
5.10A on the Outside, 5.11+	lieback	2A	C-4
Fly by Night, 5.12	face	2A	B-2
Girl's Climb, 5.10+	lieback	2	B-1
Go with the Flow, 5.11+	face	3	A-4
Grain Storm, 5.12	face	3	C-4
Greg's Crack, 5.11	offwidth	3	C-2
Greg's Face Felt, 5.11+	face	2	C-4
Greg's Face Right, 5.11	face	2	C-4

Hairdo, 5.12+	face	3	A-4
Hamburger Crack, 5.10	thin crack	3	A-3
Hammer and Sickle		5	B-4
Hard as Nails, 5.11	thin crack	2	C-4
Head First in the Bushes, 5.11+	face	2	A-4
He-Man, 5.11+	mantlel	1	A-2
Howard the Duck, 5.10+	face	2A	A-4
I Hear My Train A'Comin', 5.11+	thin crack	1	B-2
I Would Die for You, B2	thin crack	2	B-1
Jaws, 5.10+	thin crack	2	B-1
John's Crack, 5.10+	hand crack	3	C-2
Joker, 5.11+	face	2A	B-2
Korean Cowboy, B1+	mantel	2	A-4
Laverne, 5.11+	thin crack	7	B-2
Leap Problem, 5.11	face	2	B-4
Lemon Chiffon, 5.11-	face	2A	C-2
Lie Detector, 5.12	thin crack	2B	A-3
Little Horn, 5.10	face	2	C-1
Lizard Crack, 5.11	thin crack	2	C-3
Local Motion, 5.11	face	6	C-3
Long's Crack Left, 5.10+	hand crack	2	C-3
Long's Crack Right, 5.11+	offwidth	2	C-3
Long's Mantels, 5.11	mantels	2A	A-4
Magic Line, 5.10+	face	6	B-4
Manuel's Horror, 5.10-	hand crack	3	C-2
Maria's Crack, 5.9	hand crack	2A	C-4
Maria's Offwidth, 5.10	offwidth	3	C-2
Marshmallow Tower Left, 5.10	thin crack	1	A-1
Marshmallow Tower Right, 5.10+	thin crack	1	A-1
Mighty Edge, 5.11+	lieback	2	A-1
Monkey Crack, 5.10+	hand crack	3	A-4
Moroccan Menace, 5.11+	lieback	1	A-2
Mother Superior, 5.11+	offwidth	3	B-3
Mt. Everest Boulder Left, 5.10	hand	6	C-4
Mt. Everest Boulder Center, Sin Eater 5.12	thin crack	6	C-4
Mt. Everest Boulder Right, 5.9	lieback	6	C-4
Mt. Everest Boulder Far Right, 5.11-	chimney	6	C-4
Mutantis, 5.11-	lieback	3	C-3
Nancy's Offwidth, 5.8	offwidth	3	A-1
Nightmare on Elm Street, B1	traverse	3	C-3
Obsession, 5.12	face	3	B-2
Ogre, The, 5.11	hand crack	5	C-1

Outta Sight 5.9	crack	4	C-2
Painted Boulder Left, 5.10	face	2A	C-3
Painted Boulder Right, 5.10	face	2A	C-3
PHD, 5.12	lieback	4	B-4
Pickpocket, 5.10+	face	2B	C-2
Pitbull,5.11+	face	1A	A-3
Plain Nooky, 5.12	face	1A	A-3
Practice Boulders 1& 2	various	1	B-4
Pruneface, B1+	face	3	C-1
Rainbow's End, 5.12	face	6	B-4
Razor's Edge, 5.10+	lieback	1A	B-2
Retropulsion, 5.12	arête	2	C-3
Rick's Ramp, 5.10+	lieback	2A	A-4
Rick's Slab, 5.9	face	3	A-4
Ride the Lightning, 5.10	hand crack	5	C-3
Robbin's Crack, 5.10-	hand crack	2B	A-3
Rock the Boat, 5.13	seam	2B	A-2
Rockwork Orange, 5.10-	lieback	3	A-1
Rough Boys Left, B1	face	2A	A-4
Rough Boys Right, 5.11+	face	2A	A-4
Scream Seam, 5.10+	thin crack	1A	B-2
Seminar Wall, 5.11+	face	2	C-3
Sgt. Reese, 5.11-	thin crack	2A	A-4
Shawn's Knobs, 5.10	face	2	B-1
Shawn's Mantle, B1+	mantel	2	B-4
She-Ra, 5.9	face	1	A-2
Shirley, 5.11	lieback	7	C-2
Sickle Crack, 5.9	offwidth	2A	A-2
Silk Banana, B1	undercling	2B	C-1
Sin Eater, 5.12	thin crack	6	C-4
Skeletor, 5.11+	face	1	A-2
Slant Crack, 5.9	hand crack	1	A-2
Slap and Tickle, 5.11	face	1	A-2
Slapstick, B1	face	1	A-1
Snowflex, 5.10+	mantel	2	B-4
Soylent Green, 5.10+	lieback	6	B-4
Spanky, 5.11	mantel	2	B-4
Spring Break, 5.11+	lieback	4	C-4
Spud Boulder, 5.10	face	2B	C-3
Stairway to Heaven, 5.11+	face	3	C-1
Star Face Left, 5.11+	face	3	C-1
Star Face Center, 5.11+	face	3	C-1

Star Face Right, 5.11	face	3	C-1
Starving in Stereo, 5.12	thin crack	3	B-4
Substance Abuse, 5.11+	face	1A	B-2
Sunday PM Flake 5.8	lieback	1A	B-3
Syncopation , B1+	lieback	2A	A-4
Television Screen, 5.10+	lieback	1	A-1
Terminator, 5.11	traverse	2A	A-4
Test Tube, 5.11-	thin crack	5	B-3
Tips Traverse, 5.10+	face	2A	A-4
Titanic, 5.11	face	2A	C-4
Top Secret File, B1	face	1	B-1
Tower 1, 5.7	face	1A	B-3
Tower 2 Left, 5.6	flake	1	A-1'
Turbolator, 5.11	face	3	C-3
Twin Knob Mantle, 5.11	face	2A	B-4
Uncertainty Principle, 5.11	face	2	A-2
Undertow, 5.12-	offwidth	4	C-4
Vice Principal's Office, 5.12	fist crack	4	C-4
Walking on Air, 5.11	face	3	B-2
Werner's Slab Left, 5.10+	face	2	C-1
Werner's Slab Right, 5.10	face	2	C-1
Werner's Wish, 5.11-	thin crack	3	A-4
Widow Bereft, 5.12	thin crack	2	A-1
Woodward Arête, B2	arête	1	A-1
Y Crack, 5.10	hand crack	1	C-3
Zippy Crack, 5.11+	thin/lieback	3	A-31

REXRODE TRAIL

The **Cycle E. Rexrode Riding and Hiking Trail**, crossing Highway 67 just south of Mount Woodson, extends south to Lake Poway and opens access to many excellent large boulders. Peter and Eric Gomper published a small xerox guide in 1986 describing 35 boulders with climbs. These large boulders are generally top-roped crack routes of high quality. The rock is exactly the same granitic rock type as Mount Woodson. Small trails deviating from the main Rexrode Trail lead to many of the boulders, but since the area does not see a lot of traffic, they may be difficult to locate.

Directions: See the map on page 208. Park at the turnout on the south side of the road and walk a short distance to the Rexrode Trail sign. Cross the road and proceed down the trail. Generally, the boulders are on west side of the trail as you hike towards Lake Poway. Look for faint trails with red dots leading off the main trail.

Michael Paul on the first ascent of "Pruneface" (B1), Mount Woodson.
Photo by Shawn Curtis.

MAGNOLIA

Magnolia is a large hillside covered with sizable granite boulders and outcrops. The area is also known as **East Santee** or the **Lakeside Boulders**. The popularity of this area has never been extensive, although many quality face and crack routes have been done—mostly top-ropes. Boulder problems can be found in abundance in the **Spider Woman** area. A few leadable routes (**The Fin**, 5.10) have also been established on the hill. Most of the major top-rope boulders have bolt anchors.

The map below provides street access to **Magnolia, Santee, Mission Gorge, Los Coches** and **Singing Hills** bouldering areas.

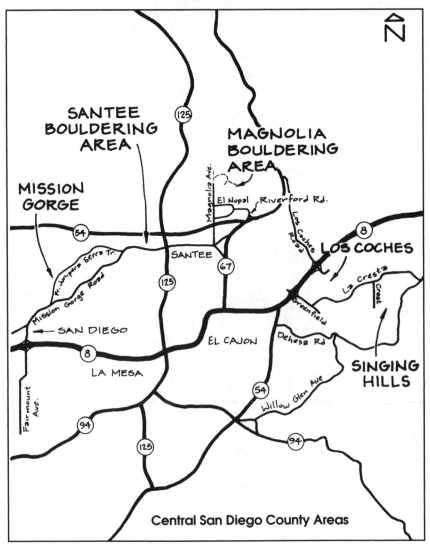

Central San Diego County Areas

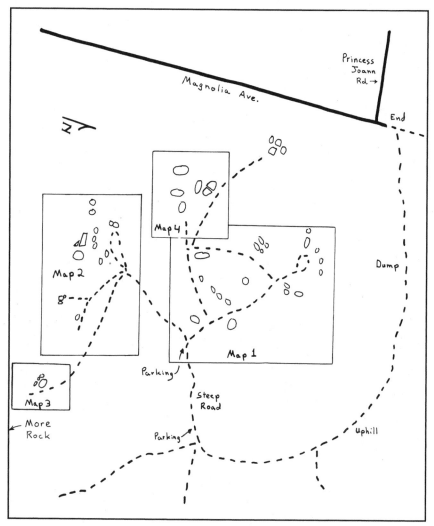

Magnolia Overview

Magnolia seems to have gone in and out of popularity with the local
scene throughout the years. A few reasons for the lack of sustained
interest include the extreme heat and dryness experienced nine
months of the year, and the abundance of other, better areas like
Woodson and Santee where there is always a local gathering. Or it
could be the graffiti, glass, and trash, along with the stripped cars
strewn over every embankment. In any event, the area is definitely
worth a couple visits and is great for the beginner and intermediate
climber.

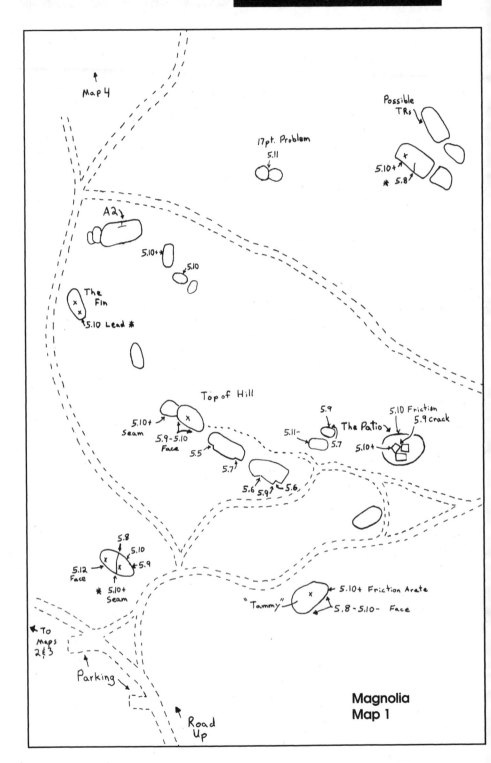

Map 4

17pt. Problem
5.11

Possible TRs

5.10+
* 5.8

A2

5.10+
5.10

The Fin
5.10 Lead *

Top of Hill

5.10+ Seam
5.9-5.10 Face
5.5
5.7

5.11-
5.7

5.9
The Patio

5.10 Friction
5.9 crack
5.10+

5.6 5.9 5.6

5.8
5.10
5.12 Face
5.9
* 5.10+ Seam

5.10+ Friction Arete
"Tammy"
5.8-5.10- Face

To Maps 2 & 3

Parking

Road Up

**Magnolia
Map 1**

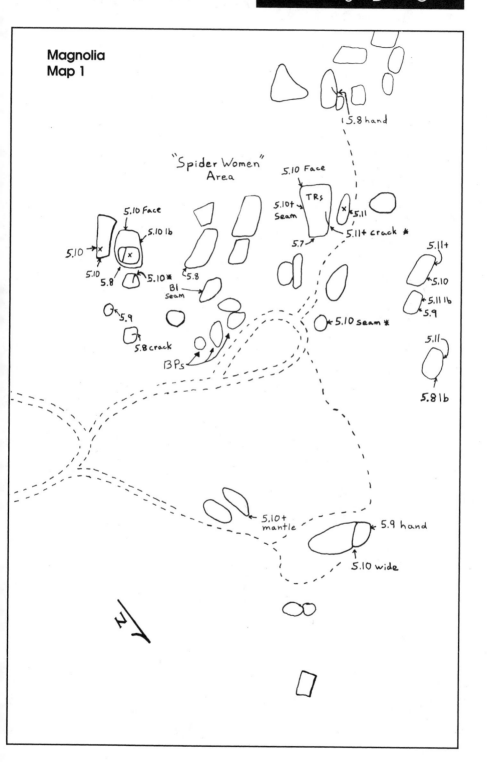

Magnolia
Map 1

"Spider Women"
Area

5.8 hand

5.10 Face

TRs

5.10 Face

5.10+ Seam

5.11

5.10 lb

5.11+ crack *

5.10

5.7

5.11+

5.10

5.8

5.10 *

5.8

5.11 lb

Bl Seam

5.9

5.9

5.11

5.8 crack

5.10 seam *

BPs

5.8 lb

5.10+ mantle

5.9 hand

5.10 wide

N

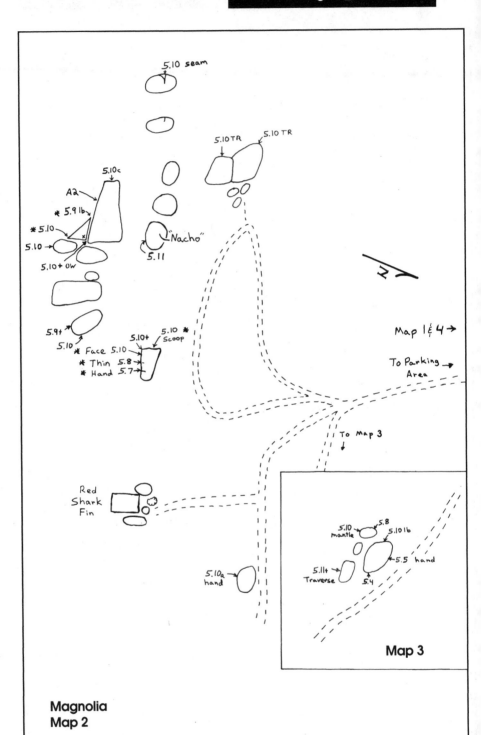

Magnolia
Map 2

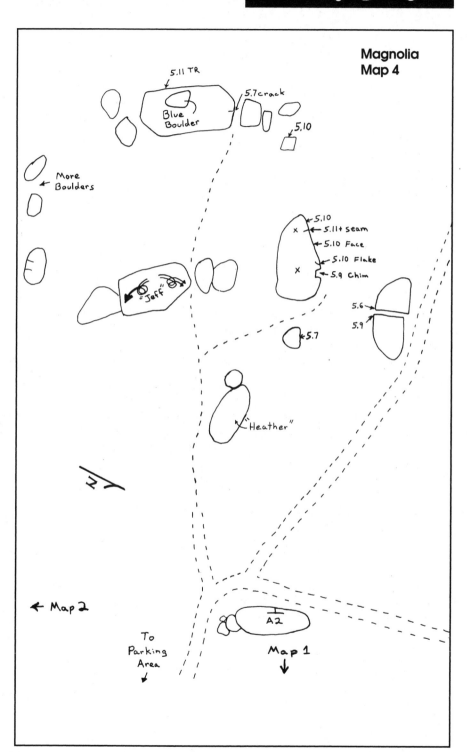

Magnolia Map 4

5.11 TR

5.7 crack

Blue Boulder

5.10

More Boulders

5.10
5.11+ seam
5.10 Face
5.10 Flake
5.9 Chim

"Jeff"

5.6
5.9

5.7

"Heather"

N

← Map 2

To Parking Area

A2

Map 1

Werner Landrey did a considerable amount of early development at Magnolia and he hosted the Great Western Bouldering Championships at this area in 1982. Dan Curley and Greg Epperson have also done considerable early exploration and development.

The area is on private property and climbers have been kicked out occasionally. Poison oak is prevalent on the north side. Some of the rocks are named after the artistic quality of the graffiti names present on the formations.

Climbing is possible year-round, but it's best in late fall, winter, and spring because the south-facing rocks bake in the summer.

SINGING HILLS

The **Singing Hills** area has become a popular sport climbing area. The area is also known as Crest and for more information see *Crest: The Climbing Guide to the Singing Hills* by David Goode. A small amount of bouldering can be found in the area besides the quality roped routes. The most notable boulder problem is a classic lieback dihedral near the summit (5.10+) called the **MiniDihedral**.

Direction: From Highway 8, take Greenfield south to La Cresta Road. Proceed up La Cresta as it turns into South Crest and make a left on Crest Drive. Turn right on South Lane and then take the dirt road in the direction of the saddle and park at the base of the hill. Walk up the hill to the boulders. **See map on page 196,** Central San Diego Map.

LOS COCHES

Los Coches Road, just off Highway 8, has abundant rock covering the hillside.

Directions: Take Los Coches exit off Highway 8 and turn right. At the road's end, park and hike up the hill to the obvious rock. **See map on page 196 ,** Central San Diego Map.

SANTEE

The **Santee** boulders are a very popular stand of large granite rocks spread out along the bottom of a hillside in the city of Santee. The rock is very smooth and rounded with the occasional thin edge or crack. The locals, with their enterprising tactics for new problems, have developed the fine art of mantelling to take advantage of the rounded, featureless boulders. Sloping mantels of every sort are found on almost every boulder and even the smallest, insignificant boulder will probably have several hard turns to satisfy the most demented mantel buff. Fortunately, face climbing routes of 10 to 40 feet are also available, many of them being top-rope climbs.

The easy access makes Santee the most popular climbing area on any given day, especially in the late evenings. The surrounding hills have been heavily impacted from dirt bikers and partiers with the usual trash and graffiti.

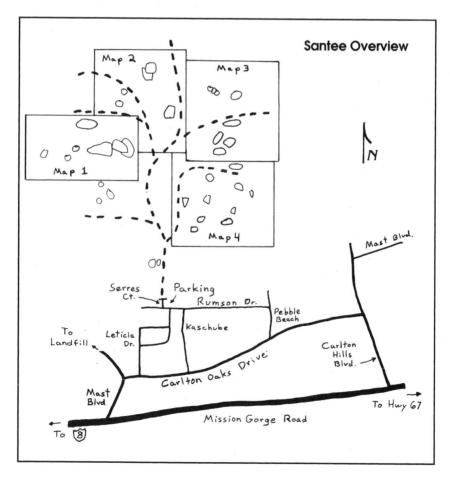

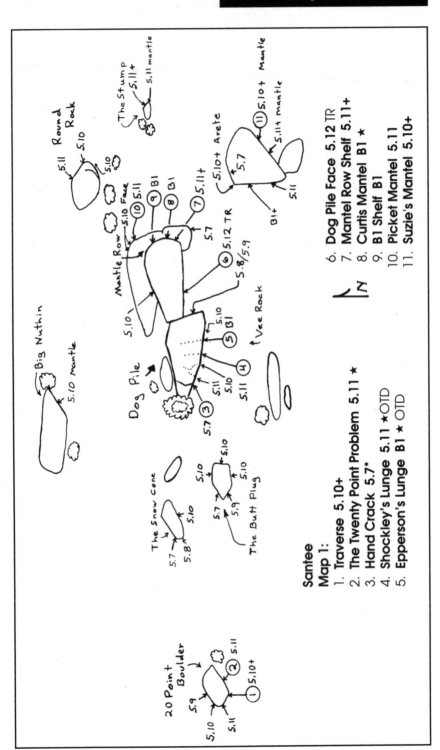

Santee
Map 1:
1. Traverse 5.10+
2. The Twenty Point Problem 5.11 ★
3. Hand Crack 5.7*
4. Shockley's Lunge 5.11 ★OTD
5. Epperson's Lunge B1 ★ OTD
6. Dog Pile Face 5.12 TR
7. Mantel Row Shelf 5.11+
8. Curtis Mantel B1 ★
9. B1 Shelf B1
10. Picket Mantel 5.11
11. Suzie's Mantel 5.10+

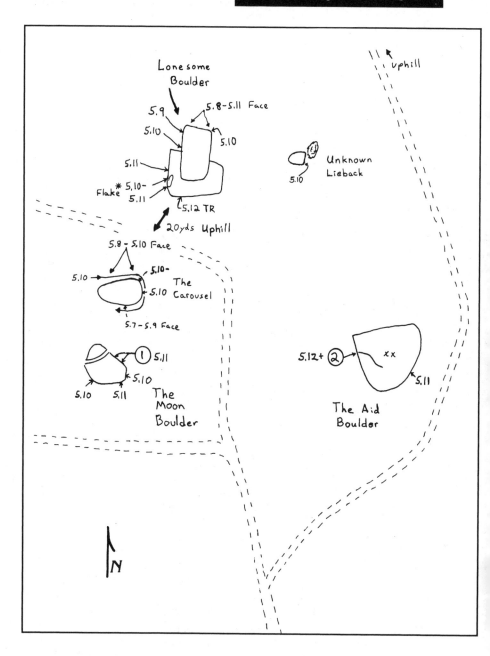

Santee
Map 2
1. **The Black Spot Problem 5.11** Left or right.
2. **The Aid Crack 5.12+** TR or lead.

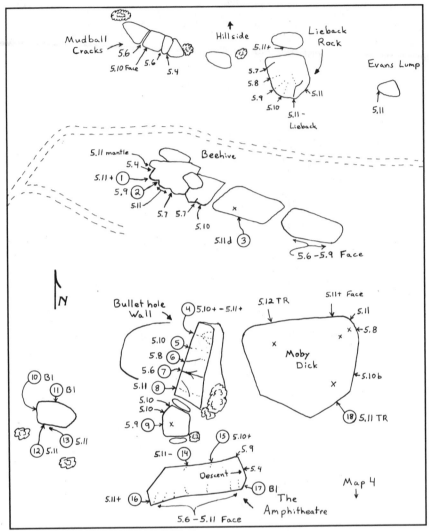

Santee
Map 3

1. **Bearhug 5.11+**
2. **Masochist Crack 5.9 ★** Hand.
3. **The Terrible Face 5.11d**
4. **Bullet Hole Face 5.10+- 5.11+**
5. **Shelf 5.10**
6. **Seam 5.10**
7. **Hand 5.6**
8. **Friction Seam 5.11**
9. **American Express 5.9 ★**
10. **Ron's Pharmacy B1**
11. **Long Tall Texan B1** Mantel.
12. **Animal Mantel 5.11**
13. **Dead Animal Traverse 5.11 ★**
14. **Powell Face 5.11-**
15. **Walkman 5.10+ ★**
16. **Jumpstart 5.11+ ★** Arête.
17. **One Cut Above B1 ★** Arête.
18. **Frerick's Flight 5.11** TR

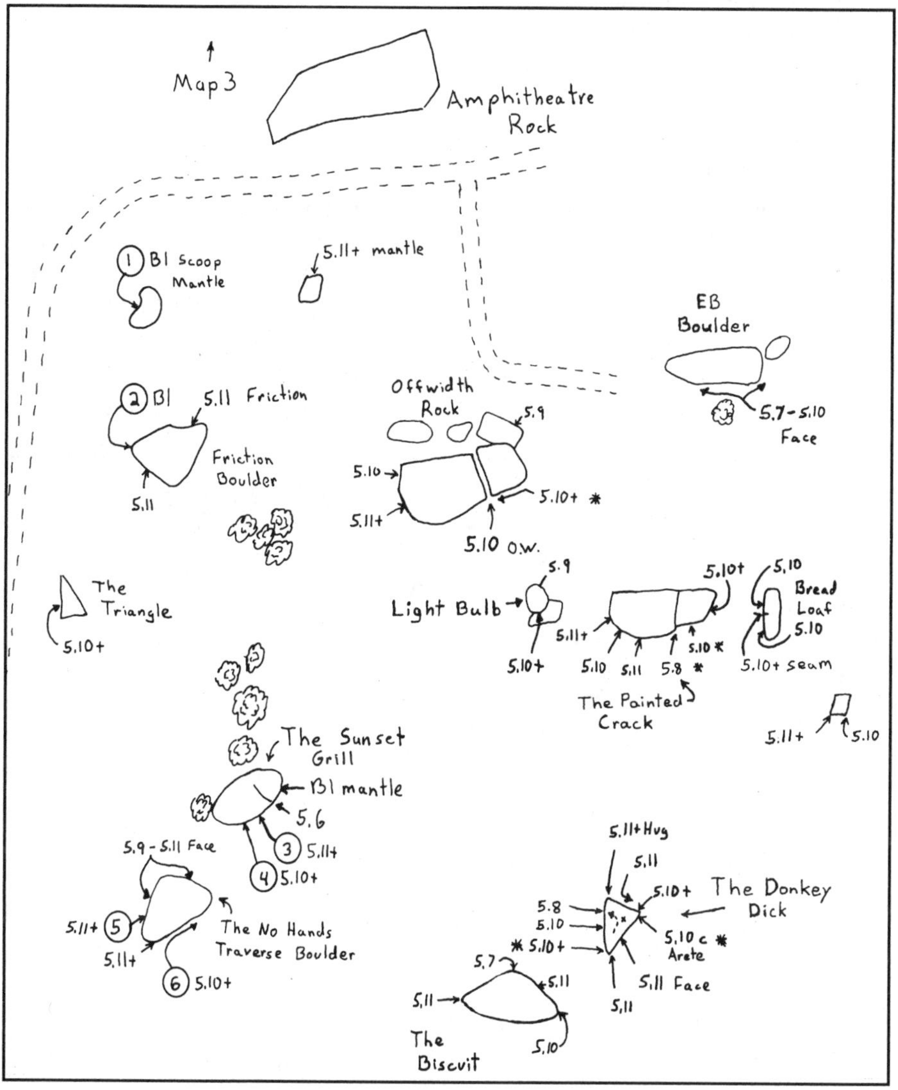

Santee

Map 4:

1. **Scoop Mantel 5.11+**
2. **Rhino Horn B1** Mantel.
3. **The Sunstroke Mantel 5.11+**
4. **The Sunset Mantel 5.10+**
5. **The Doug Moon Memorial Face 5.11+ ★**
6. **The No-Hands Traverse 5.10+**

MISSION GORGE BOULDERING

Mission Gorge is perhaps the second most popular climbing area in San Diego County, but most people come here for the excellent cragging and know little of the bouldering area that lies below the crag parking lot along the San Diego River.

The **Pink Boulder** is the large, partially submerged boulder; known for its slippery water-polished mantels. Also, problems of every sort can be found along with a B1/B1+ traverse. The **Peanut Cluster** features obscure and slippery face problems. Several other boulders shown on the map have bouldering as well.

Keep an eye on your gear and belongings—many thefts have been reported here. Also beware of stinging nettles and poison oak.

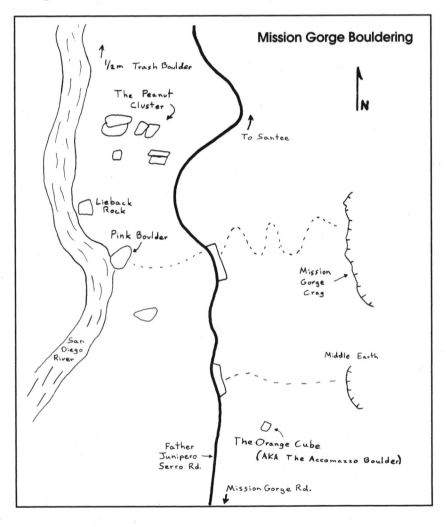

Mission Gorge Bouldering

½m Trash Boulder

The Peanut Cluster

To Santee

N

Lieback Rock

Pink Boulder

Mission Gorge Crag

San Diego River

Middle Earth

Father Junipero Serro Rd.

The Orange Cube
(AKA The Accomazzo Boulder)

Mission Gorge Rd.

LA JOLLA BEACH

The beach cliffs of **La Jolla** offer seasonal bouldering. Like **Corona Del Mar**, the climbing is very dependent upon local weather conditions, optimal conditions being low tide and sunny skies. The last few years, however, have seen the sand rise so high that many of the problems are buried. The cliffs are composed of a very gritty sandstone and sand often covers the holds. Generally, the problems are nondescript and therefore the map gives locations of areas with bouldering possibilities and leaves the route-finding up to the visitor.

The **People's Wall** is a retaining wall made of rock pieces and concrete mortar which provides an excellent 5.8 or 5.9 traverse. (Laps are usually required for aspiring sport climbers.) One can expect the usual mindless comments from tourists who just can't figure out why anyone would climb in the first place.

Possibly the best reason for going to La Jolla is to escape from the summer heat and to swim before, during, and after a pumper bouldering session. La Jolla is renowned for its beautiful sunsets and local scenery. But along with the good bouldering weather also come the crowds of beach goers that make finding a parking space a maddening affair.

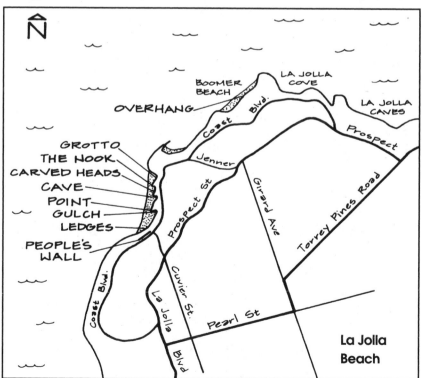

PUMP WALL

Located at Ocean Beach, **Pump Wall** is a large retaining wall that was constructed in a sectional pattern. This pattern allows for long traverses and vertical problems that utilize the gaps between the sections. The area is quite popular for after-work training sessions year-round. The piled rock at the base provides a very bad landing. Top-ropes are often used on many of the vertical problems.

Pump Wall

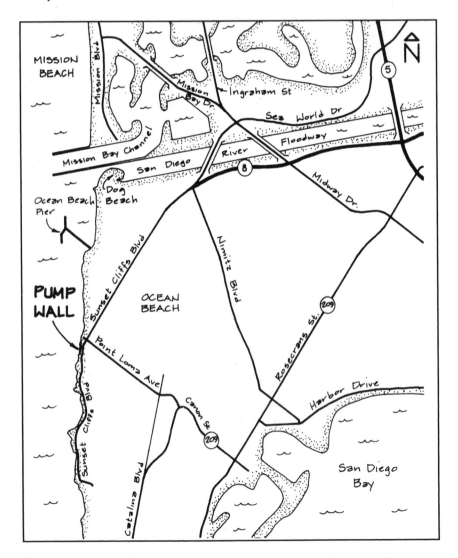

Kurt Smith and Roland Arsons on "Stairway to Heaven" (5.11), Mt. Woodson.
Photo by Mike Hatchett.

Bibliography

Amick, Ron; *Rock & Ice*, No. 13, March/April 1986; "The Santee Boulders," "Life's a Beach."

Bartlett, Alan and Evrett, Allen; *The Sierra East Side*; Chockstone Press, 1980s.

Brueckner, Keith A.; *Mount Woodson Bouldering*, 1986; Self-published.

Edwards, Steve; *Rock & Ice*, No. 55, May/June 1993; "Guide to Santa Barbara."

Gingery, Mari; *Climbing*, No. 107, April 1988; "Joshua Tree Bouldering."

Gingery, Mari; *Joshua Tree Bouldering Guide*, 1993; Quail Springs Publishing.

Gomper, Eric and Gomper, Peter; *Bouldering Guide to Rexrodes*, 1986; photocopy edition.

Gulyesh, Peter; *Off the Wall, Guide to San Luis Obispo*, 1986.

Hellweg, Paul and Fisher, Don; *Stoney Point Guide*, 1982; La Siesta Press.

Hellweg, Paul and Warstler, Hathan; *Climber's Guide to Southern California*, 1988; Canyon Publishing Company.

Katz, David; *Getting High in LA*; 1992 second edition; Self-published.

Long, John; *Climbing*, No. 98, October 1986; "J. Paul Pebble."

Mackey, Steve; *A Climber's Guide to Mount Rubidoux*, 1974; photo copy edition.

Martin, Reese; *Climbing*, No. 114. June/July 1989; "Ventura Climbing Areas."

Mayr, Troy; *Sport Crags of Southern California*, 1992; Chockstone Press.

Moser, Sally and Vernon, Greg; *Southern Sierra Rock Climbing: Domelands*, 1992; Chockstone Press.

Schaefer, Greg and Walker, Ted; *Climber's Guide to Santee Boulders*, May 1982; Self-published.

Schimmel, Carmel; *Rock & Ice*, No. 13, March/April 1986; "Mt Woodson."

Tucker, Stephen; *Climbing in Santa Barbara and Ventura Counties*, 1981; Self-published.

Van Bell, Bob; *Climbing*, No 112, February 1989; "Premium Miniatures."

Vogel, Randy; *Joshua Tree Rock Climbing Guide*, 1993; Chockstone Press.

Vogel, Randy; *The Hunk's Guide to Orange County*, 1982; Bonehead Press.

Wolfe, John; *A Climber's Guide to Joshua Tree National Monument*, 1970; Self-published.